The Sphinx and the Riddles of Passion, Love and Sexuality

Sylvia Zwettler-Otte (ed.)

The Sphinx and the Riddles of Passion, Love and Sexuality

Contributions by
Stefano Bolognini, Rainer Gross
and Sylvia Zwettler-Otte

Preface by Alain Gibeault

Bibliographic Information published by the Deutsche Nationalbibliothek
The Deutsche Nationalbibliothek lists this publication in the Deutsche Nationalbibliografie; detailed bibliographic data is available in the internet at http://dnb.d-nb.de.

Cover illustration:
Sphinx dissolving in rain © Saskia Lassmann

Library of Congress Cataloging-in-Publication Data

The sphinx and the riddles of passion, love and sexuality / contributions by Stefano Bolognini, Rainer Gross and Sylvia Zwettler-Otte ; Sylvia Zwettler-Otte (ed.) ; preface by Alain Gibeault.
    pages cm
  ISBN 978-3-631-63982-5
    1. Symbolism (Psychology) 2. Psychoanalysis. I. Zwettler-Otte, Sylvia, 1946- II. Bolognini, Stefano. „Countertransferenceless" Sphinx. III. Gross, Rainer. Sphinx as Oedipus other mother.
  IV. Zwettler-Otte, Sylvia, 1946- Three balancing acts of the Sphinx.
  BF175.5.S95S64 2013
  150.19'5—dc23

2013018978

ISBN 978-3-631-63982-5
© Peter Lang GmbH
Internationaler Verlag der Wissenschaften
Frankfurt am Main 2013
All rights reserved.
PL Academic Research is an Imprint of Peter Lang GmbH.

Peter Lang – Frankfurt am Main · Bern · Bruxelles · New York ·
Oxford · Warszawa · Wien

All parts of this publication are protected by copyright. Any utilisation outside the strict limits of the copyright law, without the permission of the publisher, is forbidden and liable to prosecution. This applies in particular to reproductions, translations, microfilming, and storage and processing in electronic retrieval systems.

www.peterlang.de

Acknowledgements

It was Rainer Gross' idea to publish our papers on *The Sphinx and the Riddles of Passion, Love and Sexuality,* which were presented and very well received in a panel of the EPF-Conference in London in 2010, and I thank him very much for his substantial support.

I am very grateful to Stefano Bolognini, the president elect of the IPA, and to Alain Gibeault, who both had contributed to the panel and now, in spite of their multiple and great tasks in the European Psychoanalytic Federation (EPF) and the International Psychoanalytic Association (IPA), welcomed our project and elaborated their valuable contributions for this publication. My gratitude also goes to the EPF-programme-committees of the conferences for providing an open space for presentations and discussions and thus for fostering our ideas within professional communities. The papers I added here were also presented at the EPF conferences in Copenhagen (2011) and Paris (2012); in their final version they owe much to the lively feed backs.

My thanks go to Gerda Schöbinger for her very helpful computer assistance, and to Helga Wolfgruber for her photo assistance.

Finally I thank Peter Lang publishing house, in the first instance Norbert Willenpart in Vienna, who is capable of kindly balancing scientific and economic interests, Stefan Tönne and Anne-Kathrin Grimmeißen, who facilitated the final process of publishing and helped to make this booklet ready for a first presentation at the IPA-Conference in Prague 2013.

Last not least I want to thank my husband for supporting me, whenever I was in danger of becoming overwhelmed by the editorial work.

Sylvia Zwettler-Otte, Vienna

Contents

Acknowledgements 5

Preface
Alain Gibeault 11

Introduction
Sylvia Zwettler-Otte 19

The "countertransferenceless" Sphinx: the narcissistic myth of impenetrability
Stefano Bolognini 31

The Sphinx as Oedipus' other Mother
Rainer Gross 39
    Freud's selection of "Oedipus material" 41
    Attempts at psychoanalytical interpretation 51
    Images of the Sphinx in art 55

Three balancing acts of the Sphinx
Sylvia Zwettler-Otte 63
    Can we solve the riddle of sexual love without killing the Sphinx? 63
    Lost Steps? – Avoidance versus use of the death drive concept 73
    Sketches in the Patient's Magic Drawing Book 87

About the authors 103

Figures 105

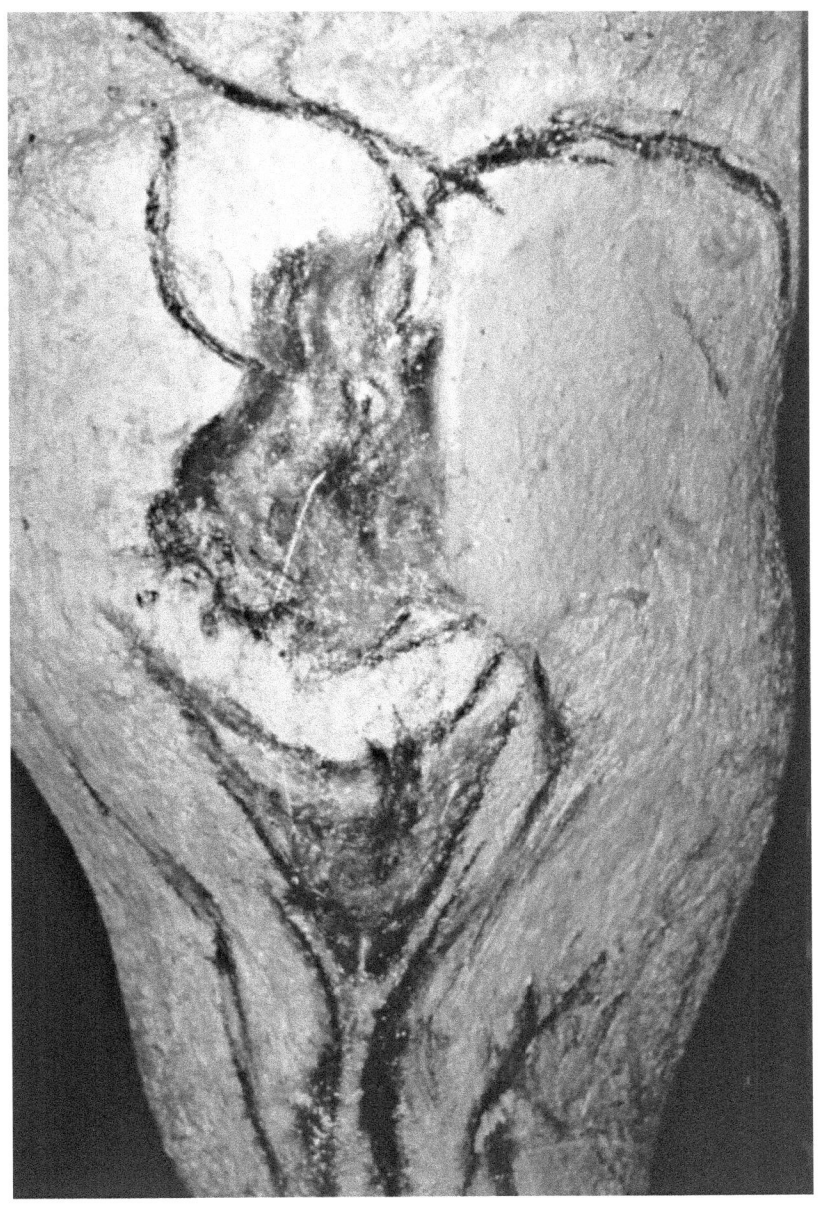

Fig. 1: Chauvet cave

Preface

Alain Gibeault

The authors of this book, Sylvia Zwettler-Otte, Rainer Gross and Stefano Bolognini, all emphasize the fact that the Sphinx is a representation of a hybrid creature, half-animal/half-human, with the body of a lion, the wings of an eagle and the head of a human being. It is interesting to note that this kind of representation plays a major role in prehistoric art, bearing witness to the very first paintings made by human beings. For example, in the Chauvet cave dating from 32000 BP (Before Present), there is a man/buffalo, a creature with a human body and hand and the head of a buffalo. If we think of the scene of the well in the Lascaux cave dating from 17000 BP, we can see a wounded buffalo facing a very schematic ithyphallic man with the head of a bird and half-leaning backwards; a stick decorated with a bird has fallen from his hands. We could interpret this scene as a realistic scenario in which a man is mortally wounded by a buffalo which is itself wounded; however, it is more probably a symbolic representation of life and death in the confrontation between man and animal. As soon as the man has established some differentiation with respect to the animal, he manifests his wish to identify with the power of the feared animal, experienced as a spirit (Gibeault, 2010).

Prehistoric art is the result of a long process of hominization linked not only to biological transformations, especially of the brain, but also to a process of humanization corresponding to the development of symbolization. In this lengthy adventure, the birth of the image is also indicative of the birth of humankind, since it shows the capacity that human beings have to represent the world in its absence. The example of psychosis shows that it is necessary to overcome the deep-seated wish for an undifferentiated union with the world in order to be able to represent it in its absence. Perception of the world supposes its previous denegation, a negative hallucination (Green, 1977), thereby creating a representational space which is at the same time a space for fantasizing and dreaming. Contrary to animals, which, according to the French philosopher Merleau-Ponty (1942), live in a state of ecstasy with the world, human beings must agree to separate themselves psychically from the world in order to create images and become more human. Humans paint images of the world to be seen, and at the same time they give birth to themselves as spectators. This is the work of mourning that lies at the heart of narcissism, in the acceptation of the difference between the sexes and between generations.

Fig. 2: Lascaux cave

In this process of representation of mankind, the scene in which Oedipus faces the Sphinx is highly significant, thanks to Freud's discovery of the unconscious and of infantile sexuality. The authors of this book have underlined in a most interesting way the many meanings of Freud's reference to the Greek myth in the tragedies and artistic representations of the Sphinx, as well as in the psychoanalytical experience. The Sphinx is thus mainly a representation of the archaic pregenital mother and of the dangers of incestuous seduction, entailing the possible death of both protagonists; it is also a representation of the wish for omniscience and omnipotence, with the fascinating and terrifying aspects that are part of these.

From this point of view, it is interesting to reflect on the mythical image of Oedipus facing the Sphinx and to compare it with another Greek myth, that of Perseus facing the Medusa: both the Sphinx and the Medusa are representations of the primitive mother-figure, but the issues involved are both different and complementary with regard to what we can understand of the psychoanalytical process.

In the myth of Oedipus and the Sphinx, there are two riddles to solve. One riddle has to do with a definition, the absence of which creates in the person who has to answer an uncanny experience: if he does not give the right answer, he is condemned to death. The answer to this first riddle is well known: "The animal that walks with four legs in the morning, two legs at noon and three legs in the evening is Man". The correct answer is thus a reference to the identity of Man. The other riddle is "Who are the two sisters who are respectively mother and daughter of each other?" The answer here is "day and night". This second question could be linked to the genealogy of the Sphinx; Rainer Gross mentions that the Sphinx is the daughter of "a dark mother goddess", the snake goddess Echidna; in mythology there would be many possible fathers. However Euripides mentions that the Sphinx could be the daughter of a mother and a daughter, Gaïa and Echidna; the second riddle would then be a metaphor of the parthenogenetic origin of the Sphinx (Pasche, 1992).

Oedipus is therefore able to overcome the seduction by the Sphinx, thanks to his capacity to give a definition of his human identity. What would have happened if he had not been able to give the correct answer? He would have been devoured by the Sphinx – there is a hint here regarding the threats entailed in the cathexis of the mother's psychical reality. Oral cathexis of the mother involves a wish to devour the object, which immediately gives rise to the fear of being devoured; an object which is both devouring and devoured is impossible to represent. This wish for an undifferentiated union with the object thus provokes the fear of confusion and a violent rejection of the object, which has been described by André Green as a "conjuration of the object" (1980). We can understand the killing of the Sphinx as an image of such a rejection; one version of how she died is not that she committed suicide, but that Oedipus threw her off the rock on which she had been sitting. This expulsion of the object, described by Freud as a withdrawal of object libido back towards the ego, leads to the annihilation anxiety that has been variously described as nameless dread (Wilfred Bion), primitive agony (Donald Winnicott), a dazzling experience of blankness (Paul-Claude Racamier), the catastrophic emptying of one's own body (David Rosenfeld), and sliding into the void of non-representation and self-annihilation (Piera Aulagnier).

However, after answering the riddles, Oedipus was not in a state of narcissistic withdrawal, but rather in a state of denial which led to the incestuous relationship with Iocasta. Gross is correct in saying that both the Sphinx and Iocasta are representations of the mother: after killing the pregenital and bad mother, Oedipus transgresses the barrier against incest and marries the genital and good mother. But as Pasche (1993) puts it, the "archaic mother never dies" (p. 121). She reappears as the plague which will render sterile all living creatures. Oedipus will have to face not only the guilt arising from parricide but also that from matricide.

However, if we refer to the issue of the riddles as a metaphor of the psychoanalytical experience, it is interesting to note that, when an analyst has to face questions by his/her patients, he/she is confronted with the same issue as Oedipus facing the riddles of the Sphinx. It is important not to answer them directly, in order not to lose one's psychoanalytical identity; for then the analyst may be "devoured" by the patient who will be encouraged to continue and ask for more answers, inducing the analyst to act out and lose his/her psychoanalytical identity. Bolognini discusses this issue from the point of view of the analyst's counter-transference, where he/she would be impelled to ask the patient questions; that too would entail the loss of psychoanalytical identity, with the analyst/analysis being trapped in a deadlock.

In order to preserve the internal and external analytical setting, it is important, as Bolognini points out, to maintain the reference to a third party. In his role as supervisor, Bolognini is such a third party between his female supervisee who is forced to be a dangerous Sphinx and her male analysand. This is also what Gross refers to when he mentions Bion's interpretation of the riddles: if the answer is not Man but a triangle, it is because only triangulation can make it possible to overcome the risks that are part of the child-mother dyad as symbolized by the relationship between Oedipus and the Sphinx. André Green has conceptualized this issue in terms of "tiercéité" ("thirdness"), videlicet: "This is why I insisted a long time ago now on the interest of a *tertiary process* and, more recently, on *the theory of generalised triangulation with a substitutable third*" (Green 1990, p. 264). What is important is the possibility of cathecting something or someone in order to create some distance between mother and child. It is only subsequently that the post-oedipal father will play that role.

If the mother's psychical reality is a threat for the child, it will be important to cathect an inanimate substance. The *sensory material* (skin appendages, clothes, jewellery) that infants place between themselves and their mother, and between themselves and their self, will be a condition of their autonomy. They can thereupon break free of the threat posed by maternal desire; as Pasche quite correctly observes: "Finding an inanimate substance, one that is soul-less – i.e. with no psychical reality – enables infants to spread out their cathexis so as not to jeopardize their self-preservation and their identity, as well as to fulfil their drives at little cost and with less risk" [1975, p. 52].

That is why the myth of Perseus and the Medusa can help us find a better solution than the one found by Oedipus confronted with the dangerous mother symbolized by the Sphinx. According to mythology, Perseus was able to defeat the gorgon Medusa by never looking at her directly – with the risk of being turned into stone – but by observing her reflection in his shield. Perseus's shield therefore has a two-fold function: that of *protection*, given that it is a barrier which separates mother and child and prevents their being merged together, and that of a *mirror* which sends out images, i.e. reflections. Pasche (1971) has developed this image of Perseus's shield as a metaphor for the work of representation necessary for overcoming the fear of non-representation and the importance of organizing a psychical space for images and words to develop. Thanks to this, man is able to become human and to master the overwhelming threats coming from the drives, as Sylvia Zwettler-Otte correctly emphasizes.

In psychosis, the individual has to deal with anxiety concerning non-differentiation. From that point of view, the psychotic is exposed to the Medusa's petrifying and immobilizing stare because he/she does not have available that protective shield against stimuli represented by Perseus's shield. Pasche [1971] describes that annihilation anxiety as being both a "break-in from the outside" and a "threat of internal explosion as a result of drive-related excess" involving de-cathexis of the external world. In order to cope with the blank that then overcomes the individual, he or she has to construct a delusional neo-reality which Pasche compares to the "phantasmagoria [...] so well described by Klein" (op. cit., p. 700), a whole series of terrifying serpents that are typical of the Medusa and compensate for the "horror of anything lacking". In a clearly Freudian approach, Pasche describes psychosis as a de-cathexis of the outside world in order to break free of a non-representable confusion with the imago of the archaic mother and as an attempt to re-cathect the world through the creation of a delusional neo-reality.

Perseus's shield as inert matter is, therefore, at the heart of the construction both of the fetish and of the transitional object. Pasche observes that the "fetish" may well be a shield, an inanimate thing that enables the individual to face up to maternal castration, but it is not a mirror, which would be able to reflect the mother's gaze. In the manner in which he explores the metaphor of the mirror, Pasche is closer to Winnicott than to Lacan, because in the experience of the mirror stage, he emphasizes the importance of the mother's gaze in which the infant can give him/herself a representation both of the self and of the world. The metaphor of the reflection in the mirror is illustrative of the importance of the function of representation as a means of surmounting the anxiety about non-differentiation that is a characteristic feature of psychosis.

Contrary to Oedipus, who was abandoned by the gods, Perseus has Athena to protect him. After cutting off the Medusa's head, which he was able to do by looking into the mirror instead of looking at her directly and becoming petrified, Perseus could make use of her head to fight his enemies and free Andromeda, and, in the end, to give it to Athena, who put it on her shield. It is not possible to destroy the Sphinx or the Medusa, but the threat that they represent has to be dealt with – not by denying their power, but by overcoming the dangers of being killed and petrified, by cathecting the world of images and words, i.e. through processes of symbolization. Thanks to *Homo sapiens*, nature has become much more controllable through the development of culture, as is so beautifully shown in the paintings of the prehistoric caves. The challenge of any psychoanalytical experience is to offer a possibility of facing up to the anxieties related to the fear of the unknown, of the imaginary and of the uncanny, without being exposed to feelings of distress and helplessness. There is a temptation to overcome these fears through omnipotent and magical solutions, but both Oedipus and Perseus bear witness to a necessary adventure, which is a work of representation of oneself and of the world, as well as that of mastering the drives and desires specific to humankind.

References

Gibeault, A. (2010): Chemins de la symbolisation [Paths of symbolization]. Paris: Presses Universitaires de France, 2010, p. 356.

Green, A. (1977): Negative hallucination. In: The work of the Negative. London: Free Association Books, 1999, pp. 274-279.

Green, A. (1980): Passions and their vicissitudes. In: On private Madness. London: Hogarth Press, 1986, pp. 214-253.

Green, A. (1990): On Thirdness. In: Psychoanalysis: a paradigm for clinical thinking. London: Free Association Books, 2005, pp. 233-278.

Merleau-Ponty, M. (1942): The Structure of Behavior. Boston, Beacon Press, 1963; London: Methuen, 1965.

Pasche, F. (1971): The shield of Perseus or psychosis and reality, in Dana Birksted-Breen, Sara Flanders, Alain Gibeault (Ed.), Reading French Psychoanalysis. London and New York: Routledge, 2010, pp. 694-705.

Pasche, F. (1975): Réalités psychique et réalité matérielle [Psychic realities and material reality], in Le sens de la psychanalyse [The meaning of psychoanalysis]. Paris: Presse Universitaires de France, 1988, pp. 43-54.

Pasche, F. (1993): Mères archaïques et subjectivation [Archaic mothers and subjectivation], in Le passé recomposé. Pensées, mythes, praxis. [Reconstructed Past. Thoughts, Myths, Praxis]. Paris: Presses Universitaires de France, 1999, pp. 113-125.

Fig. 3: Martha Bernays and Sigmund Freud 1885

Introduction

Sylvia Zwettler-Otte

It was a letter of Sigmund Freud to his fiancèe Martha that gave the idea to the papers in this book.

In April 1885 Freud had fallen ill with an easy form of smallpox and had therefore been in quarantine. He longed for comfort of Martha, complained about this unproductive time, because he had done nothing the whole days but paged through a Russian history and tortured the two rabbits in the little room where they did nothing but eating carrots and dirtying the floor. Nevertheless he has some triumph to report on April 28th:

> "But there is one plan I have nearly completed, which a particular bunch of not yet born, but born to unhappiness people will regret! Since you won't be able to guess who I mean, I'll let you in on it right away: my biographers. I've destroyed all my notes from the last fourteen years, and letters, scientific outlines and manuscripts of my work. Of the letters, only family ones have been spared. Yours, darling, were never in danger. All the old friendships and relationships presented themselves to my mind once again and silently received the chop (my fantasy still lives in Russian history); all my thoughts and feelings about the world in general, and especially about myself, were declared unworthy of survival. Now they need to be thought again, and I had written a lot. *But this stuff engulfs one like drifting sand engulfs the sphinx; soon only my nostrils would have poked out above the pile of paper;*[1] I can't mature or die without worrying about who might come across my old papers. Beyond that, everything that comes to lie before the great upheaval in my life, before our love and my choice of profession, is long dead and should not be spared a decent burial. But the biographers will need to struggle, we don't want to make it too easy for them. Each one will be right in his ideas about the 'evolution of the hero'; I'm already enjoying knowing how they will be wrong."[2] (April 28th 1885)

Freud's action – deleting material his biographers once would need, if they were to understand the development of his thoughts – might provoke a lot of thoughts, but I'll emphasize here just two points connected with Freud's two contrary directions of identifying with the Sphinx:

---

1 My emphasis.
2 I am indebted to Melanie Hart and Dr. George Brownstone for the help with the English translation of Freud's letter.

1. being passively in danger to become suffocated and overwhelmed, like the Sphinx buried in sand and
2. posing actively riddles that will be difficult to solve, like the Sphinx pressing her victims. Freud gave away to his fiancée that he enjoyed maliciously posing an enigma that was to puzzle his biographers and to make them fail.

Ad 1)

Freud's first identification with the Sphinx – the fabulous creature being half human, half animal; the suffocating drifting sand in the desert threatens to close the nostrils – is a vision of being overwhelmed in the desert, and this conveys a *contradictory view of emptiness* (desert) and *impingements* (sand in the nostrils). Actually Freud felt disturbed by old relationships, thoughts and feelings that were no longer alive, and therefore he had to get rid of them. At the same time he felt empty in the sense of being unproductive not having a special task to devote himself to. He frees himself by a deleting action and thus by becoming active he stops being overwhelmed and passive. There is also another burden at the time of his love letters: he has to struggle for earning money and for getting support and recommendations for his studies, and this humiliating situation was not in accordance with some great ideas he had. There was no chance to fight against those from whom he was dependent, but he could take revenge on posterity, fantasying how his biographers once would suffer when they would struggle to solve the riddles of the developments of his ideas. He must have assumed – like the Viennese poet Peter Altenberg in Arthur Schnitzler's tragic comedy "Das Wort/ The Word" – that

> *'posterity will be in no way better than the contemporaries, it is just later'.*
>
> (Arthur Schnitzler, Tragic Comedy: Das Wort /The Word)

Maybe Freud freed himself for some time from his resentments regarding all his obligations the scientific career demanded by imagining in a hostile way how he himself might once make others struggle as he was struggling now: 'Wait until I am great....' Thus in his daydream which he shared with his beloved fiancée, he turned molesting dependence into independence and power.

Ad 2)

Freud's passive identification with the struggling Sphinx struck me, because *we are used to identify Freud with Oedipus who solved the riddle of the powerful Sphinx*, not with the Sphinx, neither with the Sphinx who was asking riddles and devouring those who failed in solving them, nor with the suffocating Sphinx.

Fig. 4: Freud-medal with the Sphinx and Freud's picture

Ernest Jones writes (Volume II, 27) that Freud got as a present to his 50th anniversary from his pupils a medal made by Karl Maria Schwerdtner: It shows on one side a picture of Freud and on the other side Oedipus solving the riddle of the Sphinx and the Greek inscription:

> He knew the famous riddles and was the most powerful man.

This is a line at the end of Sophokles' "King Oedipus".[3]

Jones reports that Freud turned pale and felt uneasy, when he received this medal, as if he had seen a ghost. His pupils had guessed an old wish he had had as a young man: when he walked through the arcades of the Viennese University, he looked at the busts of the famous former professors and imagined that once there would stand also a bust of himself – exactly with this inscription his pupils had chosen. He seemed to be shocked that his secret wish was discovered and fulfilled.

Today you actually can see the bust with this inscription of Sophokles.

Ernest Jones provided this realization of Freud's dream: the bust was made by the sculptor Königsberger; the celebration and revelation in the arcades of the University was on February 4th in 1955. Jones stated that this was one of the seldom examples that a daydream of a young man was fulfilled in all details, though it needed 80 years.

Freud's reaction when he received the medal and the inscription are confronting us with two further little riddles that seem to have been usually neglected and that we probably cannot solve but they should at least be mentioned:

a) Why does Freud turn pale, when he receives this present? Did he perhaps have in mind the context of this Sophokles' line? It is the end of the drama: the chorus takes a synoptic look at Oedipus' fate and addresses the citizens of Thebes, inviting them to look at Oedipus who had solved the famous riddles and who had been such a powerful man, and -- who was now in deepest misfortune; therefore nobody should be praised before the end of his life. Thus Sophocles' lines are connected not mainly with praise, but with a warning. The last two warning lines are, of course, neither on Freud's medal nor on the bust, but Freud himself quoted them in the Interpretation of Dreams:

---

3 You might also notice the differences in this translation of the main line: the Greek original (see page 25) is more modest and careful speaking just of knowing, not solving the riddles...

Fig. 5, Fig. 6: Pictures of the University of Vienna, Arcades

Fig. 7: Bust of Freud

...Fix on Oedipus your eyes,
Who resolved the dark enigma, noblest champion and most wise.
Like a star his envied fortune mounted beaming far and wide:
Now he sinks in seas auf anguish, whelmed beneath a raging tide...

(Freud, 1900, Interpretation of Dreams, SE 4, 261)

So knowing the full content Freud might have felt that the fulfilment of his wish was somehow uncanny. Whatever occurred to him: it might have been a moment of opening doors to the uncanny that "destabilises our habitual way of making sense of the world" (Parsons 2009, 5). Together with the fulfilment of Freud's old wish for great acknowledgement a warning turned up. Freud wrote:

> *"[...] an uncanny experience occurs when infantile complexes which have been repressed are once more revived by some impression, or when primitive beliefs which have been surmounted seem once more to be confirmed."*

(Freud 1919, SE 17, 249)

b) The second question we might think of concerns the translations of the Greek inscription on the medal as well as on the bust.

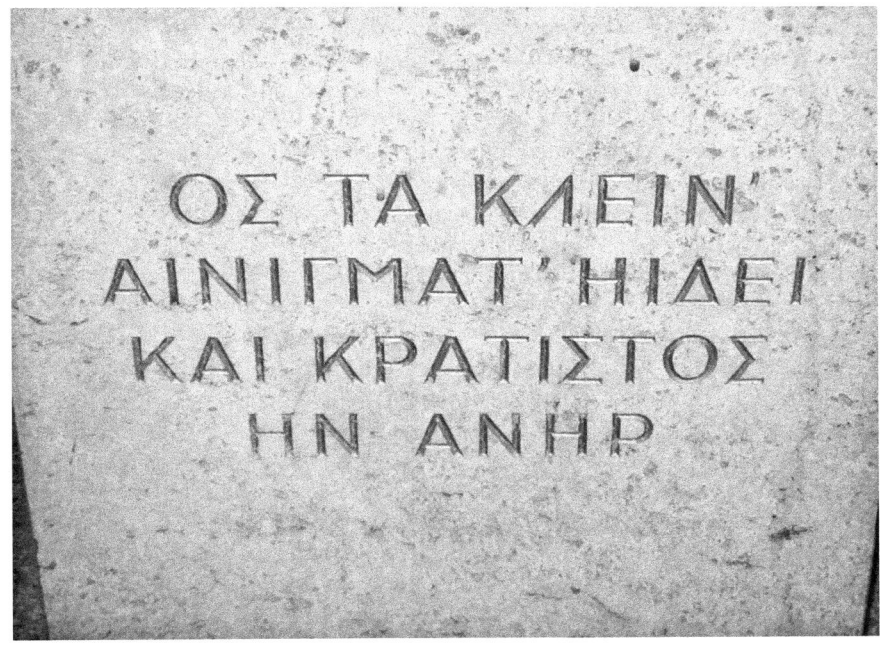

Fig. 8

The English Standard Edition (SE) and several other translations say "the riddle"- singular, while the original text of Sophocles clearly uses the plural. This might be of some relevance, if we consider Freud's interpretation of the riddle the Sphinx was asking.

Freud refers to the riddle of the Sphinx in the Interpretation of Dreams (1900, SE 4, 261) in The Sexual Enlightenment of Children (1907, SE 9,135) and in the 20th Lecture (1916-17, SE 16, 318). He takes it for granted that everyone will agree with his very short interpretation that the question of the Sphinx has as its latent meaning the sexual secret where the children are coming from

The riddle goes as follows:

'There is on earth a thing two footed and four footed and three footed which has one voice ... but when it goes on most feet then its speed is feeblest.'[4]

---

4   John Steiner, p. 118.

If we agree with Freud's interpretation it might be relevant, whether there is a plural (of children) or just a singular, since Freud assumes that the sexual discovery of a child usually starts with the disappointing arrival of another child.

Anyway, we also might wonder why Freud does not elaborate in one of these three occasions his presupposed interpretation regarding the riddle of the Sphinx which had the meaning of the Delphic oracle's injunction "Know yourself".

We have seen that Freud's identification with the Sphinx shows a development from feeling overwhelmed to becoming active. Freud's identification with Oedipus, however, contains also the *antithesis* of subjection and power and *the movement from passivity to activity*. Oedipus, confronted with the Sphinx, is in a situation of dependence; but actually what threatens him is not the Sphinx, although she is a hybrid monster made up of the parts of several animal bodies. It is his desire that causes the danger: only if he wishes to enter the city he has to pass the Sphinx and to solve her riddle. By posing the riddle the Sphinx is seductive, but it is Oedipus' decision whether he wants to take this challenge or not. Thus the danger is based on his wish to transgress a boundary. The Sphinx appears only after the parricide, as A. Green reminds us (2001, 136 f.). Oedipus has killed his father, but another obstacle to his wish arises: the imagination of a monster. It looks like the return of the fears, following the return of the repressed wish to conquer his mother. The counterpoise he has against the threatening creature is his reason that allows him to solve the riddle the Sphinx is asking him and to recognize the human development. Again the feeling of being dangerously overwhelmed is solved by starting to think and to become active.

- In the sequence Freud uses this mythological creature the Sphinx itself symbolizes the polarities of being pressed and of pressing, of *opposed instinctual aims, of passivity and activity*. She is in danger of becoming suffocated and – posing riddles – threatens to suffocate her victims by devouring them. One also might say: it is about the wish to devour (conquer the city, the mother) and the fear of being devoured – a horrible conflict. The mythological details Rainer Gross is presenting here in this book show that actually in the myth the Sphinx was traumatized herself thus living under great pressure.
- Another *dialectic view* lies – as we have seen – in Sophocles' tragedy: it ends with a warning: even the most honourable man might tip over and become a monster. The original meaning of the Latin word 'monstrum' is 'a warning sign of the Gods'(monere – admonish, warn). It is the unconscious fulfilment of an incestuous wish that is punished in this tragedy.

Freud's shift of identification from the Sphinx in the desert, becoming suffocated by drifting sand, to the Sphinx pressing her victims by posing riddles seems to invite us to take a fresh look at this mythological creature. The shift points at the contradictoriness of human psyche, and this contradictoriness is especially dominating, if we consider the riddles of passion, love and sexuality. Desire and ambivalence, symbiosis and ambiguity are issues of greatest importance through all our life. To investigate them fosters "a better understanding of problems in both normal psychology and psychopathology, and in individual psychology as well as in group, institutional and community psychology" (Bleger 2013, 3).

The Sphinx represents in a highly condensed form the imaginative psychic elaborations that the main fact of human sexuality and the force of sexual drive provoke, which is no longer confined to mating periods as with animals.

By posing a riddle the Sphinx draws a line of demarcation

– between power and subjection,
– between seductive challenge and prohibition,
– between dependence and independence,
– between boundaries and transgression,
– between guilt (parricide) and triumph and finally
– between animal-like nature and our culture.

To this book

In his preface *Alain Gibeault* refers to prehistoric art and frames the myth of the Sphinx in the process of humanization, showing the role of the image with its capacity to represent the world in its absence. He points at the Sphinx as the archaic mother, who never dies; she represents the projected wish to devour the object of desire and gives rise to the fear of becoming devoured.

In the psychoanalytic situation the psychoanalyst offers to the patient a setting that allows all these conflicts between desire and prohibition to appear and to face those archaic anxieties connected with unconscious, repressed images. In disguised and distorted fantasies very often an intrusive or devouring maternal imago can be discovered. It is experienced only in extremes: powerful, awe-inspiring, sacred, but also tyrannical, domineering and implacable, like the Sphinx, seductive and threatening. And yet she appears also vulnerable and helpless, like the Sphinx covered up to the nostrils with drifting sand. These contradictory extremes mostly coexist in alternating modes and constitute two opposite poles of the subject's own narcissistic identifications (Kohon 2010).

The patient's possessive, "devouring" wishes will be projected onto the analyst and provoke great fears to become punished and devoured.

Such an analytic experience *Stefano Bolognini, the new president of the International Psychoanalytic Association (IPA)*, is presenting in his paper "*The 'countertransferenceless' Sphinx: the narcissistic myth of impenetrability*". Bolognini followed as supervisor the treatment of a young man, who evidently experienced his analyst, a young, attractive, small and kind woman as a big, uncanny creature, like the Sphinx, unapproachable and impenetrable, with the power and the intention to reveal his weakness and insufficiency. His "impotence" extended to a broader mental aim and made him "covering his thinking with sand". In the transference he was crazed by a desire he could not express. Bolognini shows as the supervisor of "the Sphinx" impressively the long way that the patient has to go with his analyst in order "to reach the fertile and calm territory of genitality, where love and pleasure can be experienced by two separated [...] persons [...] with the freedom of feeling, sharing, and expressing reciprocal desire as one of life's riches". Bolognini also helps the "Sphinx" to face her own concerns as a young analyst, and he sees the risks of all analysts to become infected by the patient's fantasies: they might be seduced to feel really like an omnipotent Sphinx – an attitude incompatible with psychoanalytic work that needs the authentic feelings of the analyst, his 'countertransference', to come to understand what is going on in himself and in the patient.

Rainer Gross' contribution *The Sphinx as Oedipus' other mother"* refers to W. Bion and A. Green regarding the use of myths: both analysts suggest that we don't interpret a myth, but we use the myth to interpret our own problems. Thus also Freud's selection and use of the myth of Oedipus has a very personal special meaning, but also a theoretical consequence: it "enabled him to go on from seduction theory to the theory of fantasy, of the unconscious". Gross is pointing at diverse variants of the myth of the Sphinx and of the use other analysts have made of this myth. Finally he offers his own interpretation and concludes with a gallery of images of the Sphinx in art. The representations of the Sphinx differ a lot during diverse epochs. Not only sculptures and paintings are described, but also pictures created by writers and poets, and last not least by our patients, who often regard psychoanalysis or the psychoanalyst as a kind of Sphinx: "threatening and seductive, omniscient and enigmatic".

In my contribution *Three balancing acts of the Sphinx* I try to concentrate on three aspects: the struggles and conflicts between polarities, the oscillating movements between our increasing knowledge and our simultaneous unconscious denial, and our change in direction looking forward to the future and back to the past.

The Sphinx representing the dangers of incestuous seduction entails the possible death of both protagonists. This raises the question: *Can we solve the riddle of sexual love without killing the Sphinx?* In my contribution I try to elaborate some general thoughts about our culture that controls our tendencies of disorder and destruction, and about the Oedipal tragedy, which on one hand still might move us, but on the other hand often is used transformed into a banal story. An inflation of the myth dissolves the touching insight that in human sexuality desire is always transgression due to incestuous fantasies. They contain desire and boundary, seduction and prohibition, guilt and triumph – like in the Oedipal drama. Like the "Sphinx" in Bolognini's supervision also our psychoanalytic candidates shift their role from proposing problems to becoming analysts, who are trying to solve them.

Alain Gibeault has reminded us in the preface, that the Sphinx is not only a representation of incestuous seduction, but also of the wish for omniscience and omnipotence, with the fascinating and terrifying aspects that are part of these. Both wishes, the sexual desire and the "drive for knowledge" (Kohon 1999, 156), are interwoven. Psychoanalysis itself is in its essence characterized by this "overstepping of the limits of moderation", by a "threatening exuberance of thought" and therefore can hardly "be contained within the boundaries of acceptable scientific parameters". It produces with its concepts and hypotheses a "literature of excess", oscillating between consciousness and unconsciousness, a dialectical interplay, in which

> *"two different movements (are) simultaneously taking place within the act of knowing: an unconscious denial of that which has been consciously gained. Negativity, negation, disavowal are all present, as much as awareness and insight. [...] In psychoanalysis, the question is not only, whether knowledge of the unconscious is possible, but also – is it bearable?"*
>
> (Kohon 1999, 170)

An excellent example of this struggle is our hesitating and in no way uniform use of Freud's concept of the death drive, opposing Thanatos to Eros. This is the issue of *Lost steps? – Avoidance versus use of the death drive concept*. I try to show the "vacillating rhythm" of our psychoanalytic knowledge. Death is an uncanny topic. A short vignette of Hans Christian Andersen's novel "To be or not to be" illustrates the terror of dying, substituting an unmade experience. Also Franco de Masi's efforts of "Making death thinkable" are presented. Freud was well aware that his summarizing concept of the dualism of drives as binding and destructive forces would not easily be accepted; and it became rejected, ignored and avoided by many psychoanalysts. But this avoidance gives way to overlooking and acting out this very problem of destructiveness, in ourselves and in our patients. Seeing it from a positive side: using Freud's concept can be very helpful to grasp both: our professional problems as psychoanalysts as well as the silent destructiveness of some patients. In a case presentation of a female patient the concept of the death drive will help to detect an inaccessible real fear of death, the secret destruction of the self, her disobjectalisation, her dangerous hidden decathexis and its development during analysis.

The *Sketches in the Patient's Magic Drawing Book* finally present a case that shows the return of the initial phase of analysis at the end of the treatment. The patient's unconscious initial project to let the psychoanalytic treatment either succeed or fail comes up once more in the conflict between being able to end analysis and the wish to stay with the analyst for ever. Past and present events become now once more worked through. In the final phase of psychoanalytic treatment such an original hidden plan, which many patients seem to have, often reappears.

References

Bleger, J. (2013): Symbiosis and Ambiguity. London: Routledge
Freud, S. (1968): Brautbriefe. Ed. Freud E. Frankfurt am Main: Fischer
Freud, S. (1900): The Interpretation of Dreams. SE 4
Freud, S. (1907): The Sexual Enlightenment of Children. SE 9
Freud, S. (1916-17): 20th Lecture. SE 16
Freud, S. (1919): The Uncanny, SE 17
Green, A. (2001): The Chains of Eros. London: Karnac
Jones, E. (1962): Das Leben und Werk von Sigmund Freud. Bern: Hans Huber
Kohon, G. (1999): No lost certainties to be recovered. London: Karnac
Kohon, G. (2010): Amore nel transfert. Identificatione primaria e imago materna. In: Psicoanalisi, Vol. 14, Numero 2, Iuglio-dicembre
Schnitzler, A. (1966): Das Wort. Frankfurt a. Main: Fischer

The "countertransferenceless" Sphinx: the narcissistic myth of impenetrability[1]

Stefano Bolognini

For a year, I have followed Paolo's treatment in supervision. Paolo is a 25-year-old, very athletic basketball player who is obsessed with the idea that he has a small penis. This conviction makes it difficult for him to have loving relationships, and he has turned to Dr. S., whom I supervise, for psychoanalytic help after having received useless reassurances from an urologist about the normality of his genitals.

Dr. S. is a communicative woman and a nice one. She is slender and much smaller than Paolo, but he seems to have feared her from the beginning as a big, powerful, dangerous, and mysterious creature, potentially capable of pointing out his weakness and insufficiency – like all women, at any rate. The paradox is that it is precisely this woman, the one of whom he is asking help, who would have the power to confirm his impotence and disgrace.

This self-concept of Paolo's seems to extend from the sexual to the broader mental area, as though he experiences his personal "penetrance" (= capacity for penetration) as precarious and at the same time dangerous, in every situation.

And his associative process reveals this difficulty, even more so in the form of contents: Paolo interrupts his sentences halfway through, hinting at things but not completing them, as though he were "covering his thinking with sand" before it becomes clearly legible (and thus castrating himself in order not to risk being castrated by the other).

The transference, with its overdetermined inevitability and the recurrent nature of its developments, seems to be an equivalent of the Greek *ANANKE:* one cannot escape from it, despite the precautions the patient tries to adopt in order to flee from it; and the wayfarer must always risk running into the Sphinx.

The difficulty in this case is that Dr. S. is also an attractive woman, objectively speaking, which makes the situation even worse.

In fact, when Paolo enters into treatment, the first regular phase – which lasts for months – involves an obsessive lingering in Dr. S.'s bathroom while he urinates. It is as though he must thereby directly discharge "something" (aggression?

---

[1] An early version of this text was presented at the XXIII. EPF-Conference, London March 2010.

desire?), which he mysteriously feels he does not want to risk bringing into the consulting room.

The Sphinx must not notice "something" dangerous inside of him. One could say, paraphrasing the myth, that perhaps Paolo does not have a clear idea, either in his mind or in his sense of himself, of his own maturational and generational status. That is, he does not know whether he "walks on four feet" like a baby (in the sexual and mental sense); whether he is a *homo erectus (et erigens ...)*, capable of erections, desires, initiatives, and personal thoughts, as at times he comes to feel himself; or whether, in contrast, he will grow old "on three feet" without ever having loved, like the seven unhappy dwarfs of the fairy tale. The dwarfs are destined to die as childish, pregenital old people (excluded from the genital couple of Snow White and the Prince, who are instead destined to experience the fullness of love, even though younger), with their only possibility being that of excavating in the anal mine, seeking idealized diamonds/feces.

Will Paolo always need a third foot/"stick"/parent/supporting object? In short, will he forever be a prisoner of his dependence on the analyst?

The impassive Sphinx awaits Paolo in her studio, and he defends himself in the only way he knows, that is, by hiding, rendering his thoughts and emotions confusing or incomplete, sliding over his words, vaguely referring to *"one who"* or *"someone, for example",* instead of saying *"I"* – trying, in short, to escape from her.

Sometimes he moves on to a counterattack, placing the effectiveness of the treatment in doubt: identification with the aggressor (a more specific version of the transformation from passive into active) is one of the most archaic defences known. In analysis as in life, it ranges widely into still more specific categories: identification with the "abandoner", with the "denigrating disqualifier", with the "excluder", with the "confuser", etc.

All in all, there are many ways to put oneself in a safe place, and Paolo tries them all in order to overturn the situation with the fearsome Dr. S. In this he is damagingly skilful, such that I – as the supervisor of the Sphinx – must concern myself with keeping hope alive in her, hope that sooner or later something will change in this analysis, and that this elusive wayfarer could become, with time, a coherent and comprehensible person.

But the hope to do what with him? ... Certainly not to strangle him ("sphincter" and "asphyxiation" have the same lexical root as "sphinx"), or to devour him, but he doesn't know that.

One thing is sure: the mother, as an absolute, is a mysterious being, full of secrets (and secretions? ...) in which one can lose oneself. She challenges the child's penetrative immaturity, and this finds a corresponding symbolic element in the myth of the Sphinx who can be defeated only by intellect, by shrewdness – penetrative equivalents – in contrast to dull stupidity, the equivalent of castration.

Like the mother with regard to sexuality, the Sphinx can decree the "mortal" defeat of Oedipus, if he cannot "penetratively" resolve her enigmas, which according to literary tradition are classically twofold: that which alludes specifically to genitality, reserved for adults and forbidden to children and the elderly; and that relative to the alternation of day with night, which also refers to the two mothers – the solar mother of daytime, conceded to the children, and the lunar, sexual one of night-time, reserved for the father.

Paolo, in life and in analysis, feels like an anxious child who wanders about the house at night when he should be staying silent and good in his little child's bed, and instead is crazed by a desire that cannot be expressed, one that risks exposing him to derision as much as to rejection and condemnation. And Dr. S. will surely confirm this terrible reality.

It is of no use for her to remain impassive, that Dr. S! ...

It is clear that she scorns him and is ready to deride him (as though he were a fanciful little mouse in the presence of a giantess) and at the same time to condemn him (as though he were an obvious pig in comparison to a morally irreproachable person).

The object of desire, the Ideal Ego and Super Ego are all there, all three together, condensed into a single figure that scrutinizes him slyly from behind the couch.

He feels exactly like that: like a little mouse and a pig at the same time, but he doesn't even know this very well because he is completely taken up by making himself untraceable, not to be found, both to her and to himself, clouding the waters.

The young Freud, writing from Paris, sends letters to Martha that are full of idealizing, narcissistic enthusiasm (physiologically normal for his age), lavished in equal parts – as happens to all those in love – on both himself and on the object (Martha), at times with a not-so-innocent, maniacal shade to them:

> *"The bit of cocaine I have just taken is making me talkative, my little woman".*
>
> [Letter of February 2, 1886 p. 201; *Letters of Sigmund Freud, 1873-1939*]

There is the matter of his gaining acknowledgment and of overcoming his rivals in fantasy (in this letter, Nothnagel and Charcot himself), to whom Freud compares himself, denying and at the same time giving representation to his ambitions:

> *"There was a time when I was all ambition and eager to learn, when day after day I felt aggrieved that nature had not, in one of her benevolent moods, stamped my face with that mark of genius which now and again she bestows on men. Now*

for a long time I have known that I am not a genius and cannot understand how I ever could have wanted to be one. I am not even very gifted."

[p. 202, same letter]

Actually, Amalie Freud had well equipped her little Sigi with regard to his key narcissistic resources (even if Freud's interpretation that the riddle of the Sphinx is about where siblings come from constitutes evidence that his having rivals reduced his narcissistic capital). Certainly, she had equipped him better than the patient Paolo's mother had done with her son, judging from what Dr. S. and I were coming to understand.

However, even the young Freud, like all men, must give himself courage in order to confront the verdict of the "***TYCHE***" (a feminine entity).

The reinforcing resort to cocaine, confirmed in the letter in which he also speaks of Fleischl (his friend who will die of cocaine abuse), seems to be an unwitting referent even in the peculiar sentence in which he compares himself to the Sphinx semi-covered in sand:

"But the stuff simply enveloped me, as the sand does the Sphinx, and soon only my nostrils would show above the mass of paper."

[p. ix, Sigmund Freud, Life and Work, Vol. 1: *The Young Freud, 1856-1900*, London: Hogarth, by Ernest Jones]
[Letter to Martha Bernays of April 28, 1885]

This brings to mind the way in which the current generalized boom in the use of cocaine expresses the motivation put forward by many users: to strengthen their performance sexually as much as professionally. These consumers believe they insatiably want to obtain "something more", while, more times than not, they are – without knowing it – fleeing from the anxiety of *"being something less."*

The Sphinx is always there, impassive and ruthless, ready to "kill" the unprepared wayfarer and his penis/genius, and Oedipus/Freud must adapt to the performative standards of an idealized "father of the night"/Charcot; otherwise, the Sphinx's commiserating laugh at his insufficient mind/penis will destroy him.

Paolo must still work a lot, in analysis, to reach the fertile and calm territories of genitality, where love and pleasure can be experienced by two separate and sufficiently complete persons, two "great equals" (not "one great and the other little"), in the absence of winners and losers, with the freedom of feeling, sharing, and appreciating reciprocal desire as one of life's riches.

What do I say to the Sphinx during our supervision?

Well, I don't say anything very brilliant neither "genial", in fact, but I think I say things that make sense and are useful.

Along the lines of: she will have to have patience with this Oedipus who is only barely narcissistically equipped and thus still evasive; and it will be necessary to help him a little at a time in representing his fantasies and fears, in session and out, with her and with others, working them through together.

Besides, the Sphinx, too, has her fears, even though Oedipus doesn't know it. If, after some years of training, she doesn't present a well-elaborated, final clinical report, the gods will not admit her to the Olympus of the IPA, and this is no small danger!

Perhaps this contributes to making her a little impatient at times, since Paolo's performances reflect a perspective on her qualifying performance; we talk about it, and this helps "hold" the situation, broadening her already very sound capacities of containment and of working through with a colleague.

But there is a more subtle and profound problem in the background, for all analysts: the Sphinx, who is "big", who "hangs over" the ignorant wayfarer, who "knows", who is made up of a complex and elusive nature, the Sphinx could feel herself very protected by this essential difference.

In ancient Greece, to be gods or demigods offered incomparable advantages; and the intermediate figures, too, like monsters and heroes, enjoyed notable power and privileges with respect to the common mortal.

Certainly, Dr. S. has not decided on her own to be the Sphinx. If she tried, however, to blatantly deny this attribution of "dangerous" Sphinx-like intentions and characteristics brought about by the patient – either directly through her behaviour (for example, in acting "like a friend", "democratically"), or by making explicit declarations – she would not gain anything on a therapeutic level; for the patient, reassured on a conscious level that the Sphinx doesn't exist, would remain exactly the same as before (that is, terrorized) in his internal world.

Dr. S. must resign herself to *being* the Sphinx, at least for a certain time – the time necessary for mentalization and analytic elaboration of the real fantasy.

The problem is a different one and relates to the essential difference between projection and projective identification.

Paolo does not limit himself to projecting onto Dr. S. (like onto other women) a fantasized Sphinx-like profile, changing his own perception of the object: he makes the object truly *feel* that way! He sets in motion an experience, that is – not a casual one, but an intricately configured one, that can pervade all or part of the other, who in turn may or may not notice this.

If he does not notice it, the recipient unwittingly "becomes" the projectively identified character and forgets about himself, loses his own self.

Why is this important?

Because *the analyst who, inside himself, "becomes" the patient's idealized/ persecuted object, and who does not notice this, can be deeply gratified by being credited with a great deal of power*, even with great "terribleness" that on the one hand transmits omnipotence and on the other makes him lose contact with his own self.

This is not happening to Dr. S., who has a healthy sense of proportion as well as a healthy sense of humour, but I know that every analyst is tempted at some point during his professional career to indulge in letting himself go in an omnipotent fantasy, precisely when he is stimulated in this way by the patient's strong projective identifications.

What I would like to emphasize, in that insidious process, is particularly the second part of it, its consequences for the analyst's contact with *him-/herself*.

If the projective identification that is partially communicated becomes pervasive, and if it succeeds, **the analyst loses contact with him-/herself**.

An indicator of that can be that he/she no longer humbly accepts the idea that – in part, and in different proportions – the same abnormalities of the patient have been and are present in the analyst as well.

It is interesting to note that Freud's greatest discoveries, starting from the dream, stemmed from self-analysis. That is, it is really through the perception of his own complexity and his own internal difficulties that Freud was capable of comprehending and describing the human psyche more deeply than others. Cocaine has nothing to do with it! ... Freud's "scientific genitality," not the "phallic" or "non-castrated" type, was better expressed (to the point of genius) when his honesty in contacting the self was integrated with natural phallic tendencies, which granted him a useful penetrative energy, but which had also been mitigated and balanced by his internal contact with affects and fears, just as with hopes and ambitions.

In the end, it is really through the maintenance of an articulated drive complexity, and of an affective complexity, that a truly adult man can maintain his "penetrance" (capacity for penetration) without falling into the "***HYBRIS***" of incest.

Yet even today, the fantasy of "hyper-capacity for penetration" and, simultaneously, of the analyst's "scientific" impenetrability, in order to achieve the same superiority with the patient that the Sphinx had with mortal wayfarers – can subtly tempt the analyst.

One can illude to using theoretical tools, for example, that are so secure as to be able to manage the treatment in an intellectualized way, on the basis of metapsychological plans alone, *passepartout*, and with a systematizing vision "from on high," which avoids elaborative contact with the countertransference experience.

In a certain sense, the analyst-"Sphinx," who poses questions only to the other and never to him-/herself (in addition), produces the exact opposite of co-thinking and the interpsychic.

Alternatively – at the opposite end of the spectrum, and in an unbalanced reaction to a Sphinx-like stance – the analyst can welcome the pervasiveness of certain patients without any clarification of it, leading the analyst to "fall into" an identification (the true, unconscious, and substitutive one) and to lose his own identity, as happens when the concordant countertransference or the complementary one replaces the analyst's self, rather than providing him with a partial and circumscribed experience on which to reflect.

What we can work through today, better than it was possible at one time, in both ourselves and our students – thanks to the experiences and reflections of those who preceded us – is the capacity to maintain a sufficiently correct technical stance, open and neutral (in the sense of suspension), without losing internal contact with "what it is in ourselves that resonates" when we establish a deep connection with another human being and his or her problems.

It is evident that, on a theoretical level, we need not concern ourselves with "democratically" denying to the patient our inevitable external resemblance to the Sphinx; the patient's unconscious would not believe us anyway, at least for a certain period of the analysis. Our intentionally presenting ourselves as benevolent, in contrast to the Sphinx, would have exactly the same effect as the reassurances of the urologist to the patient Paolo regarding the normality of his genitals.

Instead, it will be the long, shared analytic work that progressively makes the patient see the meaning and function of the analyst's neutral suspension, with the aims of listening, exploration, and knowledge.

We must take maximal care of our internal relationship with our Self, in order to place a "whole" analyst at the service of the analysis, one who is capable of resonating with the patient's most pervasive problems, without being replaced by them, thus furthering the goal of the greatest understanding.

In a certain sense, then, we aim for "the outer Sphinx," as long as it is useful to the analytic work, but never the "inner Sphinx," if not in the sense of exploratory suspension.

All in all, I think that what characterizes a true analyst may be the capacity for suspension without losing contact with one's own complete and complex humanity.

References

Freud, E. l. (1961): "Letters of Sigmund Freud. 1873 – 1939", 1 – 478. London, The Hogarth Press.

Jones, E. (1972): "Sigmund Freud, Life and Work, Vol. 1: The Young Freud, 1856-1900", London, The Hogarth Press.

Translated by Gina Atkinson

The Sphinx as Oedipus' other Mother[1]

Rainer Gross

Let me start with Wilfred Bion's thoughts on myth in general and their function for our work: In an undated text "Tower of Babel" Bion suggests a subjective use of myths for psychoanalytic practise:

Instead of trying to interpret biblical stories of Genesis and the Tower of Babel or the fate of Oedipus he makes use of them to clarify and interpret his personal problems:

This story I do not interpret: I use it to interpret a problem of mine.

Many years later André Green generalized Bion's position and wrote – regarding the psychoanalytical attitude to all narratives:

The text interprets the psychoanalyst, not the analyst the text.

Green as quoted in Raguse 1991, p. 108

First we have to acknowledge that these mythical narratives are a social version of dreams: Emotional experiences which are transformed by alpha-function. Most of these personal myths are meaningless for everybody but the dreamer himself because the emotional experience underlying the dream is meaningful for him and him only.

But if an individual is able to transform an emotional experience of universal importance (by his individual alpha-function), if he/she can give a form to it, can communicate it in a way we are all moved by – then this man or woman is a genius according to Bion! So Bion is convinced that the myth of the Tower of Babel or Oedipus confronting the Sphinx can be used by psychoanalysts in the same way as mathematic calculus is used by scientists. The analyst should have many myths at his disposal (like the scientists many formulas), he should freely associate to them to deduce from the material of his actual patient which myth could be adequate for interpretation of the given contents. These free associations to his "selected myth" would be a form of psychoanalytic training.

So the analyst should not try too hard to document every single session. Instead of this he should write down his associations (e.g. regarding Oedipus-myth) which will be different every day.

---

1 An early version of this text was presented at the XXIII. EPF-Conference, London March 2010.

> *This procedure can be repeated, five days a week, for the same myth or for such other myths as he feels disposed to include in his canon.*
>
> Cog., p. 240

The inclusion of a myth in the analyst's personal canon, the selection as such is proof enough for the *individual* relevance of *this* special myth for *this* analyst:

> *Suppose the Oedipus myth is the chosen exercise; it will not be chosen unless it has some immediate relevance for the analyst, and its relevance must be that the analyst has an emotional experience that its either repeating, or threatening to repeat, itself. [...] This is not using conscious material to interpret the unconscious; it is using the unconscious to interpret a conscious state of mind associated with facts of which the analyst is aware.*
>
> Cog., p. 240

So Bion chose three myths to think about the problem of learning, the acquiring of knowledge:

1. The biblical story of the fall (Genesis, I, 3)
2. Tower of Babel
3. Oedipus and the Sphinx

For him these three stories were not only about sexuality but also about the tempting offer of omniscience (and therefore also about death-drive – see Zwettler-Otte: Lost steps? – Avoidance versus use of the death drive concept, in this volume).

Ad 1:

In the bible the "fall" is the consequence of the first and central temptation: The temptation of gaining omniscience.

> *... ihr davon esset, so werden eure Augen aufgetan und werdet sein wie Gott und wissen, was gut und böse ist.*
>
> *For God doth know that in the day ye eat thereof, then your eyes shall be opened, and ye shall be as gods, knowing good and evil.*
>
> Gen., I, 3/5
King James Bible

The first realisation of Adam and Eve is that of their shameful nakedness, followed by god's punishment and the expulsion from paradise. Their sexual intercourse comes later!

Ad 2.

God's prohibition to eat from the tree of knowledge, the suppression of the human thirst for knowledge by "Our Father in heaven" is repeated in the mythical story of the Tower of Babel: By destroying verbal communication between the workers God makes cooperation between them impossible: God is attacking the "linguistic link" between them!

Ad 3:

In Bion's reading the Sphinx attracts Oedipus curiosity. He is ready to pursue his search for truth at any price: So we see him in a "No win"-situation: Failure would mean plague, success means incest, suicide and death (following Sophocles' text).

Concerning the riddle of the Sphinx Bion suggests (in another undated fragment from "Cogitations") an alternative solution: The answer would not be "man" but "the Euclidean isosceles triangle!"

At first Bion's solution left me completely perplexed. Even his remark that "isosceles triangle" could be translated from the Greek as "a three kneed thing with equal legs" did not really help.

Therefore my subjective association to Bion's solution:

The invention or the erection of the triangle means gaining another (second) dimension: Before that mankind/the child is positioned in the middle of a straight line between points A und C (A and C being parts of a splitted mother image: good and bad mother).

The invention of point B as third vertex of the triangle, the invention of a third (a father) brings about the emergence from the dyadic fusion of "straight line A-C".

Of course this saving from the devouring early mother's power has a price: The bliss of the symbiotic dyad is lost forever. Nevertheless my associations led me to see the riddle of the Sphinx as an early fable, a precursor of the tale of triangulation – a task to master for every child from ancient Greece till today. Here we see myth as an "earlier mode of thinking" compared to the later development of logic and reason.

Freud's selection of "Oedipus material"

In his work and in his letters Freud was used to mention the Sphinx and her riddle as an allegory of danger: He compared Paris to a dangerous Sphinx in a letter to Minna Bernays 1885 and we all know his letter to his fiancée Martha with the image of the Sphinx of Gizeh – gladly foreseeing the problems for his future biographers by his act of burning his papers.

Fig. 9

Freud was a lifelong collector of antiquities. The Sphinx you see here is part of his collection. But it was not the only one in his consulting room. In describing Freud's daily routine about his fiftieth birthday Peter Gay described the great man's view from his chair behind the couch:

> *When he looked around his office, he saw a big picture of the Egyptian temple in Abu Simbel, a small reproduction of Ingres' painting depicting Oedipus questioning the Sphinx [...]. On the other wall he had hung a picture of the Sphinx of Gizeh: Another remembrance of mysteries – and of fearless conquerers like Freud who solved them.*

Gay, 1989, p. 197

So Freud saw a male and a female Sphinx every day for many years! His collection was not just the simple pastime of a "Bildungsbürger" but an addiction second only to his nicotine addiction (as Freud himself told his physician Max Schur). (Schur, p. 296)

He lived with his beloved figurines, his statuettes of gods and demons for decades and often used them to clarify an interpretation (e.g. the statue of Athena in the analysis of H. Doolittle: "She is perfect, but she has lost her spear …") [Doolittle, p. 94]

For Freud the mythical tales about these gods and heroes were projections of intrapsychic conflicts, externalisations, psycho-mythology. Let us now try to apply Bion's suggestion regarding the personal selection of myths to the most famous example of such a selection: Freud's "discovery" of the Oedipus myth as a perfect tool "to interpret a problem of his" [Bion, Cog., p. 226]: We can witness Freud's intellectual journey, the drama of the maybe most decisive weeks of (pre-) history of psychoanalysis in the autumn of 1897 by reading Freud's letters to his "soulmate" of these years, Wilhelm Fliess.

In February 1897 Freud was still convinced of his seduction theory and even wrote to Fliess that his own father Jacob had been "one of the perverts" [Freud to Fliess, 11.02.1897, p. 245].

But some months later this conviction – and this desire to "catch a father as originator of neurosis" ("einen Pater als Urheber der Neurose zu ertappen") [Freud to Fliess, 31.05.1897, p. 266] was shattered: Freud had begun to deal with disturbing childhood memories, recollections of desires of his own infancy surfacing in his dreams: He had begun his self-analysis and he should weave his psychoanalytic theories from the stuff of such intimate experiences. When he needed them, they came back to memory… [See Gay, 1989, p. 14]

His biographer Peter Gay states that complicated domestic relationships were wide spread in the 19th century because early death by disease or during childbirth frequently occurred – and the widowers often married again soon after. So people of different generations (not biologically related to another) lived in one house "but the riddles to solve for Freud were even more complicated than usual." [Gay, 1989, p. 13]

And now Freud had begun to struggle with his memories, his phantasies:

> *"I myself am the main patient I am concerned with. [...] This analysis is more difficult than any other. (Der Hauptpatient, der mich beschäftigt, bin ich selbst. [...] Die Analyse ist schwerer als irgendeine andere.)*
>
> Freud to Fliess, 14.08.1897, p. 281

And so his seduction theory (stating that every neurosis was caused by seduction/ abuse in external reality) had to be abandoned: In the famous letter from September 21st 1897 he wrote to Fliess that

> *Ich glaube an meine Neurotica nicht mehr.*
> *I do not believe in my neurotics anymore.*
>
> (p. 283)

And so he could no longer discern between reality and fantasy concerning the tales of his patients (and his own), because now he had

> *... die sichere Einsicht, dass es im Unbewussten ein Realitätszeichen nicht gibt, sodass man die Wahrheit und die mit Affekten besetzte Fiktion nicht unterscheiden kann.*
>
> *... the finding that there is no mark of reality in the unconscious, so you cannot discern truth from fiction which is cathected with an affect.*
>
> Freud/Fließ, p. 284

So one of the cornerstones of his thinking and clinical work of years was lost and Freud felt confused and desperate: Even twenty years later he wrote that

> *Als diese Ätiologie an ihrer eigenen Unwahrscheinlichkeit und an dem Widerspruche gegen sicher festzustellende Verhältnisse zusammenbrach, war ein Stadium völliger Ratlosigkeit das nächste Ergebnis. [...] Man hatte den Boden der Realität verloren.*
>
> GW X, S. 55
Zur Geschichte der psychoanalytischen Bewegung
>
> *"when this aetiology broke down under the weight of its own improbability and contradiction in definitely ascertainable circumstances, the result at first was helpless bewilderment. [...] The firm ground of reality was gone."*
>
> SE 14, p. 17

So for his patients and for himself he felt desperately in need of a new etiological concept to make sense of his discovery concerning the power of phantasy: Only three weeks later he had found a new solution to this riddle: He had discovered a mythical blueprint for infantile sexual and aggressive desires which became central to his thinking for the next decades:

> *Ich habe die Verliebtheit in die Mutter und die Eifersucht gegen den Vater auch bei mir gefunden und halte sie jetzt für ein allgemeines Ereignis früher Kindheit. [...] Wenn das so ist, so versteht man die packende Macht des König Ödipus. [...] Die griechische Sage greift einen Zwang auf, den jeder anerkennt, oder dessen Existenz in sich verspürt hat. Jeder der Hörer war einmal im Keime und in der Phantasie ein solcher Ödipus [...].*
>
> Freud an Fliess, 15.10.1897, S. 293
>
> *I have found, in my own case too, the phenomenon of being in love with my mother and jealous of my father, and I now consider it a universal event in early childhood. [...] If this is so, we can understand the gripping power of Oedipus Rex. [...] Each of the listeners has been such an Oedipus in his fantasy.*
>
> Freud to Fliess, 15.10.1897, S. 293 (Translation R.G.)

Of course that doesn't mean that Freud thought that there was no real trauma, no real abuse/seduction of children: This remains an important etiological factor – which was still evident for Freud even decades later (see Gay, 1989, p. 113) but: Now it was clear that there is abuse without neurosis and neurosis without abuse.

See: Marianne Krüll/Freud und sein Vater. Die Entstehung der Psychoanalyse und Freuds ungelöste Vaterbindung, Frankfurt 1979 for a critical view of Freud's use of the Oedipus myth in the process of abandoning seduction theory.

In a recent discussion the importance of both theories (of trauma and phantasy, of history and reconstruction) for psychoanalysis is pointed out by Jonathan Sklar. [2011, p. 1-28]

His very personal selection of oedipal material enabled Freud not to condemn his own father as a pervert any longer. He had to acknowledge his own infantile murderous and incestuous wishes – but: He was not the only one – his own shameful or guilty memories now could be placed in a mythical framework which showed that fantasies exactly like his own were part and parcel of the human mind, an "anthropological constant" always known to men – but described as forces active in every child's mind for the first time by Freud himself!

For his thoughts on Oedipus of course he only used a small selection of references: By choosing Sophocles' play "Oedipus rex" he took the only work where the story of Oedipus is fully told (whereas many other sources include only some remarks or sentences about Oedipus story). Alas: The prequel, the story of Laios is missing in this play! In "Oedipus rex" we are told about Laios as the victim of his parricidal son, the father's sins and shortcomings in the "pre-oedipal" story are left untold.

This selection of mythical material by Freud had its consequences: As Devereux pointed out later ("Why Oedipus killed Laios", Devereux 1953) there were other possible view points on Oedipus: Oedipus also was a traumatized child, an abandoned victim whose parents wanted him to be dead. That would have been a perfect example for Freud's abandoned seduction theory – whereas in the story Freud told (following Sophocles) Oedipus incestuous and parricidal desires come to the fore. Devereux suggested the invention of a "Laios and Iocasta complex" because he thought that the parents always try to shift all the responsibility and blame to the dark desires of their children – themselves trying to remain innocent.

In a recent paper S. Zepf and F. D. Zepf summed up the psychoanalytic speculations concerning Freud's selection of mythical oedipal material and came to the conclusion that – in reality as well as in the myth of Oedipus – "the child's oedipal conflict is the outcome of the unresolved oedipal complexes of the parental figures". [Zepf & Zepf 2012, p. 176]

If Freud had included the prehistory of Oedipus he probably would not have abandoned his theory of seduction – or vice versa. His foreshortening of the myth, his focussing on the contents of Sophocles' play enabled him to go on from seduction theory to the theory of fantasy, of the unconscious.

In the famous letter from 21.09.1897 Freud wrote to Fliess about

> ... *the finding that there is no mark of reality in the unconscious, so you can not discern truth from fiction which is cathected with an affect.*
>
> Freud/Fließ, p. 283

In the story of Oedipus there is only fiction or "mythical truths". The plural meaning that we know at least three different causes (Gods) as an answer to the question what Laios did to understand why the Sphinx came upon Thebes:

Laios was an irascible man, a character with poor impulse-control. But he himself was also traumatised like his son Oedipus: Laios' father Labdakos, king of Thebes, died when the boy was only one year. Young Laios was banned from his hometown, was forced to flee to the court of king Pelops. There he fell in love with Pelops beautiful son Chrysippos und abducted the boy, fled with him. As a consequence of that Chrysippos died (by suicide or by being killed – both tales are told). So Pelops cursed the abductor of his beloved son, put a spell on Laios: As Laios took his son away from him Laios himself should die without a son or – if he had a son – should die from the hands of his own son.

So the Sphinx was sent by the gods as an avenger, to punish Laios and his city Thebes. A reminder of the sins of the father-king, who turned away from women and from his marriage and caused the death of young Chrysippos.

The scene is set for the classical hero: A city terrorised by a monster killing all the young men. Along comes young Oedipus, saviour of city and kingdom.

In "Interpretation of Dreams" Freud gives the shortest possible account of the heroic deed:

> *Auf dem Weg von seiner vermeintlichen Heimat weg trifft er mit König Laios zusammen und erschlägt ihn in rasch entbranntem Streit. Dann kommt er vor Theben, wo er die Rätsel der den Weg sperrenden Sphinx löst und zum Dank dafür von den Thebanern zum König gewählt und mit Iokastes Hand beschenkt wird. Er regiert lange Zeit in Frieden und Würde ...*

GW II/III, p. 268

> *On the road leading away from what he believed was his home, he met King Laios and slew him in a sudden quarrel. He came next to Thebes and solved the riddle set him by the Sphinx who barred his way. Out of gratitude the Thebans made him their king and gave him Iocasta's hand in marriage.*

SE, vol. V, p. 261

Freud doesn't write one further word about the nature of the Sphinx' riddle here: She is only a beast to be slain for gaining kingdom and princess. She (or: it?) is but an object in the literal sense of the word ["object = something thrown across the path as an obstacle" in the Oxford English Dictionary]. No word about love or desire between Oedipus und Iocasta – she is just part of the prize, the trophy of the victorious warrior.

But who sent the Sphinx? The classical texts offer at least three possibilities: At least three gods were offended by the deeds of Laios:

1. Hera who wanted to punish Laios for turning away from his wife Iocasta in favour of young Chrysippos.
2. Apollo as a protector of young men and boys who wanted to avenge the fate of unhappy Chrysippos.
3. Hades god of the underworld (here the connection to Laios' sins is not so easily discerned).

Independent of these tales we are also told of

4. Dionysos sending the Sphinx out of his anger for not being worshipped in his "hometown" Thebes.

(For all four possibilities see Vogt, p. 53)

Some centuries after the invention of these myths Sophocles wrote his "Oedipus tyrannos" about 425 B.C. At his time the Sphinx already was known as a symbol of power for thousands of years. In ancient Egypt the Sphinx was male – symbolizing the supreme power of the Pharaoh by combining the body of the mighty lion with head and face of the God-King = Pharaoh. (Therefore a Sphinx commemorating the female Pharaoh Hatschepsut had a female face – with a beard!)

The most famous of these statues celebrating power is the Sphinx of Gizeh. The Egyptian Sphinx as a hybrid creature was known to all middle-eastern cultures as a mixed breed combining animal strength and the power of the human mind. This symbol of power came to Greece via Syria – sculptures and paintings of Sphinxes from Cretes Minoic culture are proof of this cultural transfer. On her arrival in Greece the images of the Sphinx show female demons of the underworld (mostly guarding tombs, sometimes carrying away dead warriors from the battlefield). In Greek art the Sphinx almost always was depicted as a winged creature (lion's body – eagle's wings – human head).

Fig. 10

These female Greek Sphinxes belong to the realm of Gaia, great mother goddess, goddess of earth, mother of Zeus. In Minoic times this earth goddess was still worshipped as equal in power to the gods of the Olympus. Some centuries later –

in the time of the classical Greek heroes of Mycenean culture – the once powerful female goddesses already were on the retreat. Gaia now was associated primarily with death and darkness as opposed to the heavenly gods of light like Athena (a virgin, not a mother goddess) and primarily Apollo.[2]

Helene Deutsch (in her lecture on "Dionysos and Apollo" from 1969) even defined Apollo as "killer of mothers". She accused him – and Greek mythology and philosophy in general – of denigration of women. The dichotomy between Apollo's realm of culture, light and reason and – opposed to that – Gaias reign over earth, nature and darkness is of utmost importance for the encounter of Oedipus with the Sphinx: He confronts the Sphinx in a historical moment of tension between the sexes, male and female forces still fighting for supremacy.

Patriarchy already ruled but there still was a threat of revenge by the overthrown earth goddess (now reduced to goddess of underworld).

Deutsch described this moment of male supremacy as a period of transition: Zeus and Apollo already reigned – interpreted as the victory of sun and light over forces of death. Apollo's most famous place of worship, the oracle at Delphi is the result of a "hostile take over" – having been a cult-place of the mother goddess in earlier times.

But – according to Deutsch – the history of Apollo only tells about a ceasefire, a short break in the fight between earth and heaven, matriarchy and patriarchy. This fight between the genders continues through the next centuries: Apollo's victory over the mother-goddess took place on a social level, not on a psychic one. After that the inner(psychic) world of men was the new battlefield.

Back to the Sphinx: The Theban Sphinx which Oedipus encountered was a special one: The mythical stories offer us some variants of her genealogy, her life-story before her death by Oedipus:

All the story lines agree in placing her in an underworldly realm, being a creature of the dark mother goddess: Her mother was Echidna the snake goddess, concerning her father there are different variants:

1. She was conceived by Echidna and the horrible Titan Typhon (Typhon was so powerful that he almost brought down Zeus. He was an avenger sent by the angry female goddess Hera – born without a father, just by a mighty strike of Hera against the earth!)

---

2   The transition from fertile mother-goddess and "hieros gamos" [meaning sacred intercourse] is an important step to the division between the realm of the sacred and sexuality which Freud called the "extraction":
    Endlich geschah es im Laufe der Kulturentwicklung, dass so viel Göttliches und Heiliges aus der Geschlechtlichkeit extrahiert war, bis der erschöpfte Rest der Verachtung verfiel. GW VIII, S. 167. Eine Kindheitserinnerung des Leonardo Da Vinci.

2. Sphinx was a daughter conceived in incest by Echidna with her own son, the hell-hound Orthos (brother of the better known Cerberus).
3. One author tells that Sphinx was married to Laios who left her for Iocasta – therefore her anger against Thebes! So she turned against the city as an outlaw, heading a band of robbers/highway-men.
4. One mythical variant even tells us that the Sphinx was an illegitimate daughter of Laios – being Oedipus half-sister!
5. Iocasta and the Sphinx were sisters (this version is reported by R. Ranke-Graves, but dismissed by most of the other scholars).

All five variants in: Vogt, p. 52

But regardless to her genealogy or motivation all sources tell about the Sphinx killing the noble and beautiful young men of Thebes (she only killed men!) and about Oedipus finally killing her.

But how did he kill her?

The earlier versions tell about Oedipus killing the Sphinx in the classical "heroic mode" by brute force: By his sword, his spear or a club.

Fig. 11

Later versions – like Sophocles' play – describe him as killing her by solving the famous riddle – killing her from the distance, by power of his word and thought![3] There is an amusing variant in which the Sphinx takes her own life by misreading an accidental gesture Oedipus made: After hearing her riddle he made a gesture with his hand, which the Sphinx interpreted (misread) as Oedipus pointing at himself – so she only thought that he had solved the riddle! [See Vogt, p. 54]

It is a bewildering fact that there are no representations, no illustrations of the Sphinx' suicide in classical Greek art! At least I was not able to find one whereas I found some illustrations of Oedipus killing her by spear, sword or club.

[There are also no pictures of the suicide of the sirens – who also threw themselves into the sea after their encounter with another "warrior of reason", Ulysses.]

Anyway: Oedipus did kill the Sphinx, the Thebans were saved from the monster, hailed him as their new king and offered him Iocasta as his wife.

Although Oedipus is one of the "early" heroes of Greek mythology (like Heracles) his story and fate changed between the times of Homeros and Sophocles: Whereas we know his tragic fate in Sophocles play in earlier texts there are happy endings for Oedipus reported too: In both Homeric epics Oedipus is just another successful hero who almost lived happily ever after: In the Ilias there is a great state funeral for him after a long and peaceful rule in Thebes (Ilias XXII, Vers 2,9 f.). In the Odyssey the suicide of Iocasta is mentioned, nevertheless Oedipus lives on as a king without blinding himself or despairing!

Attempts at psychoanalytical interpretation

I see Iocasta and the Sphinx as two opposite aspects of an internal object: The positive and negative parts of the image of an early, still almighty pre-oedipal mother. The representation of this mother must be split into Iocasta as the only good, loving and nurturing mother – and the Sphinx for the dark side of a threatening, persecutory mother trying to strangle her infant. (Sphinx = the one who strangles. Other etymological possibility: Sphinx was a term also used for prostitutes! Which could mean a seductive component of the evil mother "strangling" the young men's desire.)

---

3   Roberto Calasso described Oedipus as the most unfortunate of heroes because he was the first to kill without touching the monster – by speaking from the distance:
    The monster can forgive the one who kills it. But it will never forgive the one who did not want to touch it.
    Calasso, 1990, p. 330.
    Calasso, R.: Die Hochzeit von Kadmos und Harmonia.

So Oedipus could enjoy the bliss of symbiotic union with his idealized mother-image only after he got rid of the darker components embodied by the Sphinx.

In my opinion many contemporary philosophical works about the limits and dangers of reason and enlightenment tell the same tale: The victory of enlightenment, the triumph of male reason was and is possible only by exclusion (killing) of the irrational, threatening passions – these of course were imagined as female parts of the mind. According to the German philosophers Horkheimer and Adorno this could be one of the reasons why enlightenment and reason can lead to catastrophe – as they experienced in German Nazism! In their work "Dialectics of enlightenment" they do not refer to the Sphinx, but to the story of Ulysses and the sirens. (In their sweet song the sirens also try to seduce Ulysses with the promise of omniscience. Ulysses had ordered his sailors to bind him to the mast: So he could hear [and enjoy?] the sweet song but was unable to act upon it – and therefore survived the Siren's seductive sound.)

So the female, dark and passionate parts of the mind have to be neutralised by excluding or killing them or by forcing them to serve and adore the power of male reason: We remember H. Deutsch describing Apollo as "killer of mothers". His temple at Delphi, the place of the famous oracle was built rising over the cave of the female Pythia, who had to serve as a priestess of Apollo after his victory over the mother goddesses. (The ancient writer Pausanias described the temple frieze at Delphi: In ancient times two Sphinxes sat at Apollo's side looking up to him).

At Delphi Apollo and his priestess were responsible for riddles, for enigmatic messages to be deciphered by the faithful Greeks yearning for solutions to their personal questions and problems. Parallel to this way of gaining insight and knowledge about their individual fate there also was another Greek ritual designed to bring knowledge to the masses by emotion:

One of the most important functions of classical Greek tragedy is the gaining of insight, the change from ignorance to knowledge. Aristotle described this process as a cornerstone of his poetics by highlighting this function of ANAGNORISIS. His example for a flash of insight and a disclosure of the secret exactly at the tipping point of dramatic action is Sophocles "Oedipus rex".

So let us not forget that the tragedy of Oedipus is not only about the dangers of incest and parricide but also concerns the quest for knowledge, the danger of seeking truth at any prize![4]

---

4   In his famous book on S. Freud ("The interpretation") French philosopher Paul Ricœur also wrote about his conviction that in the Oedipus myth the question of truth and the hubris of seeking absolute truth are as important as the topics of incest and parricide. (Ricœur 1969, p. 526).

Hubris is the sin of Oedipus [...] the animal that uses action as a substitute for thought and thought as a substitute for action (not a prelude to it).

Bion, Cogitations, p. 299

At the beginning of Sophocles's play the chorus is yearning for the "sword of thought" which once enabled Oedipus to kill the Sphinx – and which will be the means of his own destruction later on when he can not solve the riddle of his relationship to his parents.

The German poet Hölderlin (who wrote a translation of Sophocles' tragedy that disturbed his contemporaries) thought about Oedipus' obsessive search for the truth: In his "Notes on Oedipus" he described the hero's "angry curiosity", which took him too far, revealed too much. In a poem he mused that maybe "king Oedipus had one eye too many ...."

150 years later André Green used the same metaphor when writing about the aggressive analytic desire to know – aggressive desire for interpretation: "the third eye of the analyst". (Green, A.: Un oeil en trop, Paris 1969)

So maybe the Sphinx is seductive not only as a dark mother-image: Her temptation could be a secret offer of omniscience, of overvaluating the power of analytic knowledge: The illusion that the solving of one riddle can give us power over the kingdom of the unconscious forever...

There are surprisingly few analytic interpretations concerning the solution of the riddle the Sphinx asked (and of the riddle of the Sphinx herself as an image):

Sylvia Zwettler-Otte wrote about Freud's interpretation ⇨ see introduction in this book.

1926 Otto Rank described the Sphinx as the phallic mother: She stands at the point of transition "from fear of mother to fear of father". For Rank the father is already represented in the Sphinx (as a "mother with a penis"), therefore her riddle is about the difference between the male and female sex.

In "The trauma of birth" Rank listed Oedipus encounter with the Sphinx as one of his numerous examples of "anxiety of birth". But he also wrote:

The father god has replaced the primal mother (who caused anxiety and lust) to create and guarantee social organisation (in the sense of Freud's "totemism").

Rank, 1924, p. 136

Theodor Reik interpreted the killing of the Sphinx as a religious replay of Oedipus' killing of his father (following Freud's "Totem and Taboo").

Reik observed that in the oldest versions of the Oedipus-story the riddle of the Sphinx is not mentioned: The Sphinx is just a terrible animal wasting the country – and therefore has to be killed by the hero Oedipus. Reik does not mention her riddle either (although the title of his paper is "The riddle of the

Sphinx"). But he defines the Sphinx as an "Angsttier" (an animal causing anxiety and panic) which shows definite signs of a mother-symbol (Reik 1920, p. 100).

German Marxist historian Borkenau offers an historical interpretation of the Sphinx and discerns three different layers:

Behind the rivalry between father and son and the incest (described by Sophocles and Freud) there is the overpowering of the mother/queen/priestess by the son in Mycenean times and – still deeper and earlier – in a third layer the ritual sexual unification of the son with mother/queen/priestess in Minoic times. (Hieros gamos – the sacred wedding)

This "three-layer-model" has interesting parallels in Freud's writings: Freud defined the pre-oedipal fate of the girl "hidden like the Minoic-Mycenean culture behind the Greek" (Freud, GW XV, p. 519) and in an addendum to "Mass psychology and Ego-Analysis" he wrote about the transitory or middle position of the heros chronologically following the age of mother goddess and preceding the father-godhead (Freud, GW XIII, p. 152).

The German analyst Rolf Vogt wrote a whole book "Psychoanalysis between myth and enlightenment or the riddle of the Sphinx" 1986:

He focuses on the parallel between human lifespan and the sun as his solution: For the Greeks the temporal aspect of morning/noon/evening was closely connected with the union between earth and sun (Helios and Gaia) in the morning, the "autonomy of the sun" at noon and the reunification of sun and earth in the evening dusk. For Vogt this is a parallel to human birth, individualisation and death.

Taking this position by Vogt one step further I would attempt to solve the riddle in describing a succession of positions:

After the end of symbiosis, the absolute emotional union with the mother in the early "adhesive position" there is individuation/gaining of autonomy /identification with the law of the father.

But: Remaining in this second position would mean a life of cold instrumental reason. (A life with maybe no symptoms, but devoid of vitality.) Only by acknowledging the inevitable dependency from objects in a "r e l a t e d autonomy" personal growth and transformation is possible! In the original text the Sphinx only tells about the **speed** of the creature "most feeble when moving on most feet". So maybe after all the "third leg" could mean not only a weakening, but a mature slowing down, an acceptance of dependency from parents and other objects – a termination of our illusion of absolute phallic autonomy!

Images of the Sphinx in art

In the art of the Romans we see numerous examples of monumental Sphinxes as a decorative element – especially for graves and mausoleums.

In Christian art the Sphinx vanished for almost thousand years probably because she was suspect as a symbol of Gnostic heresy (the Gnostics adored the Pistis Sophia – supreme wisdom, associated with the Sphinx as a symbol of old Egyptian wisdom).

In medieval times we meet sculptures of the Sphinx again at the capitals of Romanesque churches among all the other monsters. But many more Sphinxes we see in Renaissance art: Renaissance scholars and artists adored Greek and Egyptian art and culture and therefore the Sphinx was one of their favourite allegories for old and deeply secret wisdom. (E.g. in Pico della Mirandola's "poetic theology".) So we see many thinkers with beautiful and melancholy Sphinxes at their side – they were the philosopher's favourite female pet, symbolising the wisdom he could rely on (whereas it could be dangerous and threatening for uneducated people). Francis Bacon, the famous renaissance philosopher who coined the word "knowledge is power" wrote a book using famous stories of Greek mythology as allegories. ("De Sapientia Veterum" meaning "The wisdom of the elders", published 1609.) In this book he glorified the Sphinx as the allegory of science itself!

In the age of Baroque and Rococo we find hundreds of Sphinxes in the palaces and especially in the baroque parks and gardens. They are all beautiful, mostly with proudly erected breasts and sometimes their faces show the features of the king's or prince's mistress (so you can admire a Sphinx with the face of Madame Pompadour in the park of Versailles).

All these sculptures and pictures show beautiful, maybe enigmatic creatures – none of them threatening in the least.

But at the same time we find examples of the darker and more dangerous aspects of the Sphinx in literature of the 17th and 18th century: The greatest writer of German language, Johann Wolfgang von Goethe (adored by Freud), writes exactly about the horizontal splitting of the Sphinx (beautiful face and upper body, dangerous lower body and genital) in Faust II: His hero Faust is searching for the most beautiful woman in the world, Helen of Troy and therefore his personal devil Mephistopheles leads him to the classical "Walpurgisnacht". There they meet the Sphinx and even Mephistopheles is scared by her sight:

Du bist recht appetitlich oben anzuschauen.
Doch untenhin – die Bestie macht mir Grauen

Your head and bosom make a pretty show,
What horrifies me is the beast below.

Faust II, 2. Akt, Verse 71/46-47

About fifty years later the eminent romantic poet Heinrich Heine wrote his poem "The Sphinx" as a celebration of a dark, seductive woman bringing death to her lovers.

In 1894 Oscar Wilde wrote in his poem "The Sphinx": "Terrible animal, you are raising all my animal instincts".

There is no equivalence of this dark threat in the visual arts: Many pictures through the centuries show a melancholy young thinker confronting an enigmatic Sphinx. In these images there is no sign of violence or sexuality to be seen. Oedipus does not have to kill the Sphinx, she is no danger to him but a beautiful and melancholy partner in philosophical dialogue. I consider this to be an example of aesthetisation as a defence! And this defence mechanism was not only applied by the artists of the 18th and 19th century, it still seems to be at work: We all know the vignette of the famous painting by Ingres depicting a pensive Oedipus, a young philosopher in front of a peaceful Sphinx: You can see this drawing on every front page of the International Journal of Psychoanalysis till today!

Fig. 12

The powerful Egyptian Sphinx was "starring" in many Hollywood-films and is well-known in popular culture till today: For example we see a "funny" story depicting the aggressions against the most famous of Sphinxes in "Asterix and Cleopatra", a volume of the very popular French cartoon which is also widely read in German speaking countries.

We see Asterix and his dumb friend Obelix adoring queen Cleopatra and especially her very beautiful nose. Being in Egypt Asterix and Obelix visit the Sphinx of Gizeh – like millions of tourists today. And dumb Obelix just has to climb the giant Sphinx. Climbing up on her huge stone face he "accidentally" demolishes the nose of the Sphinx (displacement of a castration of the feared phallic mother? But: Did Obelix "know" that the Sphinx of Gizeh was a male Sphinx?). Therefore the nose of the Sphinx of Gizeh is missing – although (or maybe because) it was so very special for Asterix and Obelix – almost as beautiful as the nose of Cleopatra, the good mother giving them presents and being saved by them. Our two Gallic warriors support the good mother Cleopatra against her lover, the "evil" Cesar.

Through the centuries it is maybe easier to hear/read about dangerous aspects of the Sphinx (passions) compared to the dangers of actually seeing these threats! But this aesthetic defence seems to break down in the second half of the 19th century: The symbolistic painters show us many dangerous Femmes fatales, they indulge in depicting La Belle Dame sans Merci or other seductive female forces: These creatures still are beautiful, but now their sensuous beauty *is* the danger! Gustave Moreau's Sphinx calmly sits on a rock full of dead young men – her victims. The Sphinx in Khnopff's picture is a lascivious cat in heat.

Fig. 13

Maybe there was a parallel to the age of classical Greece two thousand years earlier: A patriarchal society undermined by the threat of uprising of the suppressed forces of female sexuality and power. The spell of the seductive and threatening mother was felt again in Fin de siècle Vienna: In the pictures of that time the Sphinx with her beautiful face seems very close to the image of the "beautiful Iocasta".

We all know Freud's answer to that "Zeitgeist". In the same Fin de siècle-years and in the same city a famous writer chose a different approach to the Sphinx: About 1904 Hugo von Hofmannsthal wrote his play "Oedipus and the Sphinx" as a celebration of dangerous sensual seduction. In his text Oedipus and the Sphinx are close to incestuous intercourse (in an early draft he even wrote that Oedipus did sleep with the Sphinx – but he did not dare to show that on stage).

His Oedipus doesn't speak a word in front of the Sphinx, she just kills herself after calling him by his name. Oedipus stumbles down the mountain into the arms of Iocasta, who speaks out the "Leitmotiv" of the play:

> *Die Mütter ziehen alles hinter sich. Die Welt hängt an den Müttern ...*
> *The mothers – they draw everything behind them. The whole world is hanging on to the mothers ...*

Hofmannsthal, p. 148

In this tragedy Oedipus and Iocasta do love each other – in an atmosphere of brooding sensuality this can only be a love to death.

So many men thought about the Sphinx and her riddle during the last two thousand years. But what about the women? Could Oedipus solution of the Sphinx' riddle be an example of what we call "gendered discourse" today?

In his paper "Gendered discourse – discourse on gender" Roy Schafer wrote about the Sphinx being an empowered und potentially dangerous woman (in Greek mythology) relative to the power-hungry male adventurer, the boy seeking manhood. Implicitly she has made Oedipus pay for his "phallic" answer, "Man".

Schafer reports a woman's version of Oedipus and the Sphinx: The poet Muriel Rukeyser tells the story in her way:

> *Long afterward, Oedipus, old and blinded, walked the roads. He smelled a familiar smell. It was the Sphinx. Oedipus said, "I want to ask one question. Why didn't I recognize my mother?" "You gave the wrong answer," said the Sphinx. "But that was what made everything possible," said Oedipus. "No," she said, "when I asked, What walks on four legs in the morning, two at noon and three in the evening, you answered, Man. You didn't say anything about women." "When you say Man," said Oedipus "you include women, too. Everyone knows that." She said, "That's what you think"*

Muriel Rukeyser, quoted in Schafer 1997, p. 54

So for thousands of years the Sphinx as a symbol and an allegory stays enigmatic: She is a creature in between.

Between the wisdom of old Egypt and the rationality of classical Greece, between the male and female sex, between threat and seduction, between superhuman divine wisdom and subhuman animal passion, between prohibition of knowledge and transgressive omniscience. (See also Zwettler-Otte's paper "Can we solve the riddle of sexual love without killing the Sphinx", in this volume.)

In the fantasies of many of our patients today – and in the opinion of the general public for more than hundred years – psychoanalysis is also regarded as a kind of Sphinx: Threatening and seductive, omniscient and enigmatic. And the inventor of psychoanalysis, Sigmund Freud? Having disclosed so much about himself in his writings and letters – and still remaining an enigmatic Sphinx?

As an old and sick man Freud was forced to identify a last time with Oedipus: This time not with "Oedipus rex" but with "Oedipus at Kolonos". He also was forced into exile, like Oedipus seeking dignity on his death bed he also had to flee not to Athens but to London with his very own Antigone: Anna. There he could at least die in freedom surrounded by his beloved antiquities.

Will we be able to develop enough "negative capability" to endure our state of not-knowing? Is it possible for us to "remain in uncertainties, mysteries, doubts, without any irritable reaching after fact and reason"[5] even in situations of danger, in threats, in the "war on psychic terror"? Can we avoid to think and interpret too quickly when facing a "riddle of the Sphinx"?

Maybe we should remind ourselves that there will always be a tension in analytic practice between reasonable distant "Apollonian" technique and unreasonable, emotionally entangling "Dionysian" forces of the unconscious.

When we interpret the whole story of Oedipus and the Sphinx as a dream – so that all the protagonists would represent dissociated parts of the dreamers mind – maybe then it could be possible not to kill the Sphinx by solving her riddle once and for all times. As psychoanalysts we continue to shift in every session between intrapsychic distant reasoning and "unreasonable" close contact of unconscious impulses between analyst and patient. Both of them (analyst and patient) will continue to oscillate between identifications: They will be identified with Oedipus as riddle-solver – and with the Sphinx and her dangerous and seductive riddle.

Therefore every solution of this riddle must be provisional, cannot be permanent because (to use Bions favourite quotation from Maurice Blanchot[6]) "La

---

5 Bion quoted this definition of "negative capability" from a letter by the poet John Keats to his brothers George and Thomas (written on December 21st 1817).
6 Bion told 1976 that "Dr. André Green once drew my attention to the quotation from Maurice Blanchot ..." [Bion 1994 b, p. 307].

réponse est le malheur de la question." Bion translated: "The answer is the misfortune of the question" and added:

> When you don't know the answers – a desirable state of affairs if every session is to be an entirely fresh one – you have to find new words.

Bion 1994 b, p. 287

References

Bacon, F. (1990): Weisheit der Alten (Hg: Rippel, P.), Frankfurt: Fischer
Bion, W. R. (1994 a): Cogitations, London: Karnac
Bion, W.R. (1994 b): Clinical seminars and other works. London: Karnac
Borkenau, F. (1957): Zwei Abhandlungen zur griechischen Mythologie. In: Psyche XI, 1, p. 1-27
Calasso, R. (1990): Die Hochzeit von Kadmos und Harmonia. Frankfurt: Insel
Cherry, J. (Hg.) (1997): Fabeltiere. Von Drachen, Einhörnern und anderen mythischen Wesen. Stuttgart 1997, Reclam
Demisch, H. (1977): Die Sphinx. Geschichte ihrer Darstellung von den Anfängen bis zur Gegenwart. Stuttgart: Urachhaus) 1977
Deutsch, H. (1973): Dionysos und Apollo. In: Die Sigmund Freud-Vorlesungen. Frankfurt, p. 9-64
Devereux, G. (1953): Why Oedipus killed Laius: A note on the complementary Oedipus complex. Internat. J. Psychoanal. 34, p. 132-141
Doolittle, H. (1976): Huldigung an Freud. Rückblick auf eine Analyse. Frankfurt/Main: Ullstein
Freud, S. (1986): Briefe an Wilhelm Fließ 1887 bis 1904 (Hg: M. Masson). Frankfurt: Fischer
Gamwell, L. and Wells, R. (ed) (1989): Sigmund Freud and art. His personal collection of antiquities. New York: H. Abrams
Gibson, M. and Néret, G. (2011): Symbolismus. Köln: Taschen-Verlag
Goscinny, R. (1969): Asterix und Kleopatra. Berlin/Köln: EHAPA
Kerényi, K. (1984): Die Mythologie der Griechen, Band II: Die Heroen-geschichten. München: dtv
Heinrich, K. (2007): Dahlemer Vorlesungen 3: Arbeiten mit Ödipus. Begriff der Verdrängung in der Religionswissenschaft. Frankfurt/Basel: Stroemfeld
Heinrich, K. (2001): Dahlemer Vorlesungen 7: Psychoanalyse Sigmund Freuds und das Problem des konkreten gesellschaftlichen Allgemeinen. Frankfurt/Basel: Stroemfeld
Hofmannsthal, H.von, (1968): Ödipus und die Sphinx. In: Ödipus Band II. München /Wien 1968, Langen-Müller (p. 89-180)

Horkheimer, M. und Adorno, Th. (1988): Dialektik der Aufklärung. Philosophische Fragmente. Frankfurt: Fischer

Raguse, H. (1991): Leserlenkung und Übertragungsentwicklung – Hermeneutische Erwägungen zur psychoanalytischen Interpretation von Texten. In: Z. für PA Theorie und Praxis, VI, 1991, p. 106-120

Rank, O. (1909): Der Mythos von der Geburt des Helden. Leipzig/Wien: Deuticke

Rank, O. (Original 1924): Das Trauma der Geburt und seine Bedeutung für die Psychoanalyse. Frankfurt 1988: Fischer

Reik, Th.: Ödipus und die Sphinx. In: Imago VI, 2, p. 95-131

Ricœur, P. (1969): Die Interpretation. Ein Versuch über Freud. Frankfurt: Suhrkamp

Schafer, R. (1997): On gendered discourse and discourse on gender. In: Schafer, R.: Tradition and change in psychoanalysis. London: Karnac (p. 35-56)

Simon, E. (1999): Ödipus als mythische Persönlichkeit im Bewusstsein der Antike. In: Ödipuskomplex und Symbolbildung (Hg: Weiß, H.). Tübingen, Edition diskord (p. 20-47)

Sklar, J. (2011): Landscapes of the dark. History, Trauma, Psychoanalysis. London: Karnac

Sophokles (1973): König Ödipus (Übersetzung von Schadewaldt, W.). Frankfurt: Insel

Steiner, J. (1993): Two types of pathological organisation in Oedipus the king and Oedipus at Colonus. In: Psychic retreats (p. 116-130). London: Routledge

Van der Sterren, D. (1986): Ödipus nach den Tragödien des Sophokles. Eine psychoanalytische Studie. Frankfurt: Fischer

Vogt, R. (1986): Psychoanalyse zwischen Mythos und Aufklärung oder das Rätsel der Sphinx Frankfurt: Campus

Zepf, S. & Zepf, F.D. (2012): „Man bittet, ein Auge zuzudrücken" – Von Freuds Verführungstheorie zur Theorie des Ödipuskomplexes und zurück. In: Zeitschrift für PA Theorie und Praxis, Heft 2, p. 152-180

Three balancing acts of the Sphinx

Sylvia Zwettler-Otte

The Sphinx, half animal, half human, represents the human struggles and conflicts between drive and reason, desire and fear, seduction and prohibition and many other polarities. She is a representation of our efforts to balance between contradictory options.

"[…] walking on wire between the Twin Towers is both horrifying and fascinating", Adam Phillips introduces his essays about balance (Phillips 2011, XI). In the following three parts I'll try to show this ambiguity involved in three aspects: the struggles and conflicts between polarities, the oscillating movements between our increasing knowledge and our simultaneous unconscious denial, and our change in direction looking forward to the future and back to the past.

Can we solve the riddle of sexual love without killing the Sphinx?[1]

In a touching letter of Freud to his fiancèe Martha he identifies himself – not with Oedipus – but with the Sphinx asking riddles[2]. To give the right answer to the Sphinx was a question of life and death and had the meaning of the Delphic oracle's injunction 'Know yourself!'

Some years later, after Freud had discovered that we all might recognize our own desires in this myth, he identified himself with Oedipus. This shift of identification from the Sphinx to Oedipus raises further questions like: Has sexual love always to do with transgression? Why has the Sphinx to die, when the riddle is solved?

These questions might be essential for our psychoanalytic work, since the process of cure is bound to a relapse of the patient's secret love-story. Moreover, our candidates have to shift their role from being patients who first are proposing problems (like the Sphinx) to becoming student-analysts who are trying to solve them (like Oedipus).

---

1 An early version of this text was presented at the XXIII. EPF-Conference, London March 2010.
2 See Introduction.

Culture contains all those achievements that control our tendencies of disorder and destruction, it encompasses our compromises between our conscious and unconscious desires on one side and our rules and prohibitions aiming at canalizing them on the other side. Human sexuality, different from the sexuality of animals, is characterized by a constant force of sexual drive, and on this constancy the powerful elaborations of our imaginations are based (Green 2001, 221). With other words: The line of demarcation we are looking at is the border between sexuality that we can watch also in animals, and psychosexuality that is enriched and burdened with our human elaboration of sexuality. It is an elaboration freight with fascination and fear. While fascination can serve as a guideline in pursuing our aims and desires, fear keeps us back, makes us observe the limiting rules and observe the prohibitions. When our anxieties increase and threaten to overwhelm us, the object of our sexual desire might become alienated and resemble rather an animal than a human being: an attractive woman might be transformed into a dangerously seductive Sphinx, thus shifting the desire from oneself to the other.

The myth of Oedipus arrogating the capacity to solve the riddle of the Sphinx has the meaning of transgressing a boundary. Thus it is a triumph and attacks the power of the Sphinx. It is a triumph of reason that seems to be incompatible with the life of the monster. The riddle brings death either to those who cannot solve it or to the Sphinx who is defeated, and jumping into the abyss she commits suicide.

I have already mentioned in the introduction that Freud did not elaborate his short interpretation of the riddle of the Sphinx. Thus Freud's interpretation demands our own continuation of his thoughts. Freud wrote that "The sexual interest of children begins by turning [...] to the problem of where babies come from – the same problem which underlies the question put by the Theban Sphinx – and it is most often raised by egoistic fears on the arrival of a new baby." (Freud 1916, SE 16, 318) With three concrete pictures the riddle supposes the human development: the upright grown-up is followed by the old man with a stick and preceded by a crawling baby. The prolongation of this line of development would in both directions provoke a frightening picture: birth out of the female genital on the one side, death on the other. But of course, birth is the answer to the children's question where the little rivals come from. It forces our look at the female genital that provokes fascination as well as fear according our fantasies. Michael Parsons wrote:

> *"To give significance to the sexuality that brought one into existence and to the death that will take one out of it is a lifelong psychic work. Being fully alive means being able to do this, by dynamic après-coup and avant-coup, in such a way that both origin and extinction can resonate with meaning in one's life today"* (2009, 14).

As Freud wrote in the "Interpretation of Dreams", the Oedipal drama confronts us with

> *"our inner minds, in which those same impulses, though suppressed, are still found. The contrast with which the closing Chorus leaves us confronted – strikes us as a warning at ourselves and our pride, [...]. Like Oedipus, we live in ignorance of these wishes, repugnant to morality, which have been forced upon us by Nature, and after their revelation we may all of us well seek to close our eyes to the scenes of our childhood" (But the tragedy of King Oedipus) "moves a modern audience no less than it did the contemporary Greek one, [...due to] "the particular nature of the material"*

(Freud 1900, SE 4, 262 f.).

Today it is still valid that Oedipus' tragedy can have a touching effect on us, although our ways of defences against it might have become multiplied. But also the sexual liberation which had a lot of consequences for the individual and for the society, could hardly "affect the Oedipal unconscious fantasy, the unconscious psychic scenario, the incestuous fantasies", Gregorio Kohon pointed out in 1986, and he added:

> *"The Oedipal drama has been transformed into a totally banal sequence of 'events' and 'anecdotes': everybody can talk – and even joke – about it. But the joke is on us: what makes sexuality in human beings specifically human is repression, that is to say, sexuality owes its existence to our unconscious incestuous fantasies. Desire, in human sexuality, is always transgression; and being something that is never completely fulfilled, its object cannot ever offer full satisfaction"*

(Kohon 1986, 370 f.).

Some years ago the latent meaning of the myth of Oedipus has become more differentiated: the classical view had been that Oedipus defeated the Sphinx and accepted the offers of the grateful city: to become the king of Thebes and marry the recently widowed Jocaste; without conscious knowledge that she was his mother and that he had killed his father. According to a newer interpretation by John Steiner, who followed the ideas of the classicist Philip Vellacott, these facts were both known and unknown at the same time to Oedipus who turned a blind eye to the unwelcome reality because of his desire to enjoy the throne of his father and the bed of his mother.

Steiner wrote: "Oedipus adopts a state of mind which can be thought of as a psychic retreat from reality and a defence against anxiety and guilt" (1993, 129). The retreat from truth was supported by others who colluded denying reality each with their own separate motives. But the plague possibly representing the corruption led to the need to begin the struggle to face the truth. In worst case turning a blind eye, which is based on a pathological organization, can result in a total retreat from truth to omnipotence: reality is dismissed and "alliances with omnipotent figures" are made in order to control destructiveness and cruelty. "The individual is then possessed by monstrous forces, and since these contain projected parts of the self a complex structure results" (Steiner 1993, 130).

In the Sphinx we can see these monstrous forces that appear overwhelming and dangerous. The Sphinx appears as a monster, thus alienated in a double way: she is not human, but an animal, and she is not a normal animal, but a hybrid monster that reminds us of diverse dangerous threats with the parts of several animal bodies.

All these components allude to important features of the human experience of sexual love:

- There is the animal-like force of drive that might become overwhelming. The conception of the sexual drive as a foundational, biological term emphasizes that we can rely on sexuality as a basic psychic organiser, but reducing sexuality, as it was understood by Freud, to genitality would result in a conceptualisation that would let us miss some crucial components. "Sexuality is characterised by peremptoriness and drivenness; one talks of the sovereignty of sexual desire and passion" (R. Stein,1998, 254), nevertheless we seem to be again and again in danger to loose what makes sexuality play such a central role in psychic life. When we speak of 'passion' we are alluding already to the aspect of becoming overwhelmed, of suffering and of being prohibited from satisfying our desires or being endangered and punished. The force of the superego is fighting against the force of the drive.

The human elaboration of the experience of sexual drive contains seduction and prohibition, desire and boundary, guilt and triumph.

- Prohibition, boundary and guilt lead us to the question of the aim of limits. They might be reasonable and aim at preventing damage. But they might also intend to suppress and demonstrate the inferiority of the person who is inhibited in her activities.

The consequence of prohibitions and taboos is that we are put to the test: shall we respect the prohibitions or shall we try to transgress them? Where desire is dominating, there will be the will to transgress. In the Oedipal drama the Sphinx obstructed the way into the city. Posing a riddle was in itself a seduction to transgress this limit. Oedipus was ready to do so. It was a risk for him, but also for the Sphinx who was not able to bear that the riddle was solved and her illusion of power was destroyed. But Oedipus' had the same fate: after his triumph he could enjoy his sovereignty for a long time, but then his illusion of power was destroyed, too.

The myth of Oedipus became in our European culture the most famous example of transgression out of incestuous wishes. Incest, however, is not limited to European culture, but exists in some form everywhere: a certain constellation of the relationship becomes prohibited in the family thus defining what is considered as transgression.

The anthropologist Georges Bataille (1963, 180) wrote that there are two things that cannot be avoided: dying and transgressing, and according to him both coincide. He called the human being the only animal that does not only accept nature, but negates it also.

Longing for *continuity* the human being is confronted with discontinuity, because there is an abyss between the human beings; by their erotic desire and their reproduction power they try to transgress the abyss.

In her paper "The poignant, the excessive and the enigmatic in Sexuality" (1998) Ruth Stein elaborates valuable insights and "some palpable truth" (260) for us analysts gleaned from Bataille's formulations. She points out that according to Bataille we long to re-establish the lost continuity in order to escape our lonely separateness. This desire is expressed in the quest of eroticism, but in a flow of coalescence and renewal, like the ebb and flow of waves surging into one another, the self is dispossessed. Looking with another human being into the abyss that lies between them, aims again at a union; the joint look results in a shared feeling of dizziness. Our ideas about death represent

> *"a deeply regressive and transcendental wish to let go, a 'desire to go keeling helplessly over what assails the innermost depths of every human being. Thus desire to give oneself up is at the same time a desire to live to the limits of the possible and the impossible with ever-increasing intensity"*
> *(Sexuality can be seen)* *"as the greatest secret, the symbol of enigma and hidden truth."*
>
> (Stein 1998, 256; 258).

This fresh light on sexuality in Bataille's presentation brings back to us, what we again and again seem to repress: a basic experience of sexuality that contains paradoxes, conflicts, pain and subversive power and can seem to us monstrous because of the vehemence and irrationality of eroticism. Human awareness demands a calm ordering of ideas, but this capacity is easily destroyed by primordial violent feelings. When reason succumbs to violence, it is a movement that exceeds the bounds – it is an excess. Ruth Stein suggests that adults pre-consciously sense the disruptive emotional power of eroticism and therefore try to keep it a secret from children. Erotic desire triumphs over taboo, and this joy of overcoming is deeply different from animal sexual need.

Stein illustrates this aspect of radical difference of eroticism from ordinary life and work by a vignette of an analysand. This woman remembered her "first kiss" from a boy as great confusion, she could no longer understand, why she should continue going to school and why people go on working, after they have experienced "this absolutely wondrous, otherworldly sweet thing"; she felt clearly the gap that separates that world of unspeakable pleasures from daily activities which now seemed suddenly pale to the point of meaninglessness. These feelings could in analysis be traced back to incestuous feelings towards her forbidden and seductive father and finally to her lost first love object, her rejecting mother. The first kiss was for her a benign penetrative act and repaired some of her archaic fears of being penetrated and wounded by the paternal destructive persecutory penis.

Fascination of pleasure and prohibition transpose the individual into a state of mind that allows him to transgress his limits of a separate existence and to satisfy his longing for merging and losing himself. This brings about ideas to equate Eros and death. Prohibition appears to be necessary because of the limited condition of human existence and because of the impossibility of returning to the primary and pre-oedipal state. Desire originates as prohibition, and prohibition defends against the impossible. *"The prohibited and the impossible are two different dimensions of the "No", the barriers that eroticism seeks to overcome"* (Stein 1998, 260). Thus taboos and prohibitions protect not only society and culture, but are also a defence against the painful feeling of the impossible and of experiencing one's smallness. Sexuality provides in its tendency and capacity for excess the experience that for some moments it might be possible to transgress the boundaries of separateness. To this power sexuality owes its exciting, vitalising and invigorating effect.

Considering these polarities we might understand that human sexuality is a force containing opposing tendencies regarding adaptation and survival.

In regard to the question what transforms sexuality into psychosexuality we are confronted with the enigma of the Sphinx that has to do with lifting oneself up from our four legged position.

Laplanche showed that the power of sexuality bridges bodily excitations and sensations with the enigmatic, sexual message from the unconscious of the caregiver. Stein pictures Laplanche's thinking on sexuality as a tension arc between bodily excitations, and curiosity and questioning evoked by the mother's unconscious sexuality, between the own body and the fantastic object, between inside and outside. *Sexualisation serves not only as a defence, but it is also a capacity and an achievement regarding the excess influx of stimuli and the experience of a gap. Human sexuality is the desire for the lost object and expresses the human need for overstepping one's boundaries.*

Fig. 14: Greta Garbo-Sphinx

Focusing on prohibition, boundaries and transgression we are in midst of the Oedipal drama. But the Sphinx as any fabulous animal-like creature can also represent an earlier regressive stage with its sexual wishes and fears regarding internalised object relations with all the deep needs and conflicts involved. And this might even lead us further back to pre-oedipal anxieties: working with our patients we might often find behind sexualisation "silent, deep-rooted shapes of distress" (Stein 1998, 254).

We can realize that we don't have the slightest chance of getting a glimpse of the riddles of sexual love and passion, if we forget about those aspects that can appear monstrous to us when curiosity and fascination succumb to prohibition and fear. 'Monstrous' then gets the meaning of animal-like and dangerous, not human. As soon as we call it 'uncanny', we might recognize our efforts to alienate, what is secretly familiar to us. Seduction and petrification might appear (Figure 14: Greta Garbo-Sphinx, C. Sinclair Bull).

We have not necessarily to look for a monstrous creature like the Sphinx; there are other "monsters" much easier to find in our everyday life. Stefano Bolognini described in his booklet "Like Wind, like Wave" thoughtfully and with humour what we are inclined to project into animals. Bolognini tells us in these 'Fables from the land of the Repressed' about his experience with dogs: he had learned "to love and respect them without fearing them" (p 8.), even if they look as dangerous as the giant, lion-like Caucasian sheepdog. He invites the reader to reflect what we learned from Freud about phobias (like that of little Hans regarding horses) and of his essay about the "Wolfsman", and he shows the symbolic meaning animals can have based on our unconscious associations. He points at Melanie Klein's descriptions of the processes of splitting which enables us to make contact with lost parts of ourselves that became projected outside. And he reminds us of Heinz Kohut's "discovery, deep down on the ocean bed of our unconscious, of the remains of the archaic grandiose self, which was shipwrecked like the Titanic at the first hard impact with reality" (p. 12). Based on these general human condition Bolognini also provides us with an empathic image of the analyst's hard work, when he sometimes – trying to contact a patient suffering from his isolation and mental hunger and thirst (p. 71) – might feel like someone who bravely climbs up a tree beyond all safety limits to help a desperate cat to come down again and in doing so has to battle with that deadly frightened silly creature "resisting rescue with clawing and scratching" (p. 74). In all these stories we find a deep understanding of our task to establish contact with the wilder and more diffident elements and parts of the self, of ourselves (Bolognini 1999).

Concluding my contribution the question whether sexual love has always to do with transgression has to be answered in the affirmative. Sexuality involves excess and transgressing the limits we are used to. When reason succumbs to passion and peremptory feelings, this means a movement that exceeds the boundaries and belongs to "our intrapsychic movements, working in the direction of ideas surrounding lack, absence, passion and longing for the irrational and impossible" (Stein 1998, 257).

Considering sexuality as a bridge and a 'tension arc' opposed poles become connected: body and fantasy, pleasure and pain, fascination and fear, familiar and strange – a contradictoriness we are used to in our psychoanalytic way of thinking. When Stein following Bataille referred to the intimate connection between religion and sexuality, she mentioned also the etymological root of the word "sacred": it has the meaning of set apart (from daily affairs), holy, but sacrè in French denotes sacred and – in vulgar parlance – also damned.

We can add to this the following:

Freud himself dedicated to this phenomenon an impressive essay: "The antithetical meaning of primal words", where he picked up the peculiarity the philologist Karl Abel described: in the oldest languages a fair number of words have two meanings, one of which is the exact opposite of the other. Freud wrote: "I did not succeed in understanding the dream-work's singular tendency to disregard negation and to employ the same means of representation for expressing contraries until I happened by chance to read a work by the philologist Karl Abel, which was published in 1884..." (Freud 1910, 153 f.) The solution of the riddle of the antithetical meaning of primal words is that our concepts owe their existence to comparisons; for instance, we cannot distinguish light without having an idea of dark. Later on the two sides of an antithesis can be separated and hence it can be thought of one without conscious comparison with the other. "Sacred", derivate from the Latin sacer, is one of these old words that kept this antithetical meaning.

> *I suggest that the antithetical sense of words intends to find some orientation in regard to an object: is it helpful or dangerous, will it provide pleasure or pain, is it good or bad? Thus it is very near to and linked with internal conflicts. It is the question of maturity and integration, whether we can grasp, that one and the same object can have good and bad meanings as well, and that it can change its meanings.*

This leads us finally back to the title: Can we solve the riddle of sexual love without killing the Sphinx? We might answer: it depends.

It depends whether we are able to perceive the Sphinx differently; of course, then the Sphinx will no longer be a dangerous monster representing external objects we are afraid of, parts of ourselves we prefer to see outside of us. This is exactly what the psychoanalytic process facilitates and what Loewald (1960, 225) called a "new discovery of objects, and not discovery of new objects, [...] a new way of relating to objects as well as of being and relating to oneself."

Thus the death of the Sphinx might be transformed and reduced at least to a sleep[3] – since nobody can be sure whether there will not be another moment in his life where a monster is raising again its head. Perhaps we should return to Sophocles' notion regarding Oedipus: – the line which is on Freud's medal and his bust:

> He knew the famous riddles and was the most powerful man.

That he KNEW about the great enemata means a reduction: 'knowing' is more modest and careful than solving riddles.

We have started with Freud's shift of identification first with the Sphinx in the desert endangered to become suffocated by drifting sand, quickly erected to the Sphinx posing riddles, and then with Oedipus who solved the riddle of the prohibiting and threatening Sphinx. In analysis we hope that our patients also can pursue such a development from being overwhelmed to a more mature and active way of living and relating to objects after the relapse of their secret love-stories.

Finally I want to think of our candidates: their shift from passivity to activity is even more evident. Bolognini stressed that the training of our candidates "is not so much a process of formation as one of *transformation*" *(Bolognini 1999, 75)*. After psychoanalysis has helped them to come into contact with their own monstrous parts and to confine them, they might no longer feel seriously overwhelmed; they might become ready to shift their role from proposing problems (like the Sphinx) to becoming analysts who are trying to solve them – or at least to know about them (like Oedipus.)

References

Bataille, G. (1957 <1963>): Der heilige Eros. Neuwied am Rhein: Luchterhand
Bolognini, S. (1999): Like Wind, like Wave. Fables from the land of the Repressed. New York: Other Press
Freud, S. (1900): The Interpretation of Dreams. SE 4
Freud, S. (1907): The Sexual Enlightenment of Children. SE 9
Freud, S. (1910): The antithetical meaning of primal words. SE 10
Freud, S. (1916-17): 20th Lecture. SE 16
Green, A. (2001): The Chains of Eros. London: Karnac
Jones, E. (1962): Das Leben und Werk von Sigmund Freud. Bern: Hans Huber
Kohon, G. (1986): The British school of psychoanalysis. London: Free Association Books

---

3   Also the fairy-tale of the Sleeping Beauty transforms death into sleep.

Loewald, H. (1986): Psychoanalyse: Aufsätze 1951-1979. Stuttgart: Klett-Kotta
Parsons, M. (2009): Between Death and the Primal Scene. (Unpublished manuscript).
Phillips, A. (2011): On Balance. London: Penguin Books
Stein R. (1998): The poignant, the excessive and the enigmatic in sexuality. IJP, Vol. 79
Steiner J. (1993): Psychic Retreats. London: Routledge

Lost Steps? – Avoidance versus use of the death drive concept[4]

> "Pasos perdidos doy sobre la tierra, pues todo es aire ..."
> Lost steps I am taking on earth, because everything is air ....
> (**Lope** Félix **de Vega** Carpio, 1562-1635)

I.

Whether we are thinking of *steps* forward or upward – it is about a *movement*.

The notion 'step' contains both, the idea of a *movement* and of a *rest* as well (if we think of the steps of a stair). And it includes opposed directions: moving *forward or back, upwards or down* – anyway, changing places.

On *some* steps it might be a *matter of choice* where we go.

There is the risk, that we treat inconvenient concepts as "stepchildren"[5] we would like to ignore or dismiss. But if there is nevertheless truth in such discoveries of unconscious mechanisms, they will remain effective without being recognized, and they will influence our *anxieties and methods*:

- our own conviction regarding the potential of psychoanalysis
- our concepts and methods of understanding and treating our patients and candidates,
- our attitude against environments, whose critics and hostility is and was always easier to see than their (unconscious) needs and requests,- a fact which might have to do with our persecutory anxieties – and

---

4 An earlier version of this paper was presented at the EPF-Conference 2011 in Copenhagen.
5 Susann Heenen-Wolff coined at the EPF-Conference in Copenhagen the term "Freud's stepchildren" for rejected psychoanalytic hypotheses or concepts.

- our efforts to prove ourselves worth and compensate for the lack of wished for evidence of psychoanalysis – a wish which is understandable, but this does not necessarily mean that it can be fulfilled, as Gregorio Kohon pointed out as a main speaker of the EPF-Conference in London 2010.

In "Beyond the Pleasure Principle" (1920) – the most important paper for our thoughts about the death drive – Freud speaks of the "Zauderrhythmus": which is translated "vacillating rhythm". Etymologically "zaudern" (hesitate) is not quite clear, but seems to be connected with "ziehen" (pull), "gelingen" (succeed), while vacillate (from Latin vacillare – stagger, waver, German: wanken) is close to emptiness (Latin: vacuus). Thus also the languages seem to mirror the oscillations between moving in a certain direction and losing it. "It is as though the life of the organism moved with a vacillating rhythm. One group of instincts rushes forward so as to reach the final aim of life as swiftly as possible; but when a particular stage in the advance is reached, the other group jerks back to a certain point to make a fresh start and so prolong the journey" (Freud 1920, SE 18, 40 f.).

My hypothesis is that we are in a similar rhythm oscillating between discovering truths and losing them again, because we hardly can avoid choosing our methods according our anxieties and our needs. An eminent example is Freud's concept of the death drive, of the dualism of the instinctual drives.

As Quinodoz pointed out regarding "Beyond the Pleasure Principle" – this "turning-point in Freud's thinking" (Quinodoz 2005, 185) remains also today a highly controversial concept: "We could almost say that there are as many opinions as there are psychoanalysts" (Quinodoz, 2005, 193). In my view, this impression depends on the question which point of the oscillating movement we come to see. Are we just stepping forward or back again?

A very important German contribution by Joachim F. Danckwardt (2011) is in my view a big step forward. It is called "The Denial of the Death Instinct" (Original: Die Verleugnung des Todestriebs). By collecting unjoint parts of theory before and after 'Beyond the Pleasure Principle' Danckwardt shows how far-reaching Freud had further developed the life-death-instinct-hypothesis and how the death drive concept contributes to an understanding not only of destruction, but also of new formations in structural processes.

The vacillating rhythm in our psychoanalytic knowledge is a peculiarity and essential of psychoanalysis, an ongoing struggle between awareness and negation. This peculiar quality of psychoanalytic knowledge derives from the negativity from which the unconscious is constituted. It results in the impossibility to exclude one's "own passion for ignorance from the act of knowing". Not even Freud himself could "escape the combined action of disavowal and the splitting of the ego", as Kohon showed giving a few examples (Kohon 1999; 164). He wrote:

> *"There always seem to be two different movements simultaneously taking place within the act of knowing: an unconscious denial of that which has been consciously gained"*
>
> (Kohon 1999, 170; see also introduction in this volume, p. 29).

Stepping forward and back again – these oscillations hardly can be avoided. This is also the reason, why I suggested that we should no longer concern ourselves with the so-called "crisis" of psychoanalysis, as if it were a dangerous critical *moment*. Instead, it might be more helpful to accept the fact that there are permanent internal movements and struggles, past and present, which are also, of course, reflected in and act upon external reality.

Thus we might return to the original meaning of the Greek word crisis, as it is used in the oath of Hippocrates: *as our capacity to discriminate*, which does exist, although in a limited way.

The original meaning of the Greek word "κρίσις", as it was used in the oath, obliges the physician to act

'kata dynamin kai k r i s i n emen',
i.e. "according to my power and my capacity to decide".

There has been a noteworthy shift from the active meaning in the original Greek "crisis" to a passive connotation in our use of the foreign word "crisis" nowadays. The original meaning of "krisis" contains both: the fact of our human capacity to influence our fate, *and* our limitations. (Zwettler-Otte S., 2005; 2006 and 2009; a short version was published in EPF Bulletin 2004, 58.).

Freud was aware that his summarizing concept of the dualism of drives opposing Eros and Thanatos as binding and destructive forces would not easily be accepted. He may have felt some hesitation himself, because he finished "Beyond the Pleasure Principle" in May 1919 and kept it back until July 1920, but he became "more and more convinced of its validity" (Quinodoz 2005, 186)[6].

It might appear obvious, why one neglects the concept of the death drive. *Like all human beings*, psychoanalysts are prone to fear of death, incapable of imagining it and avoiding what provokes fear. (R. Fliess, 1956,6) And rationalisations of avoiding the topic of death are easily at hand, as Susann pointed out in 2003: many followers Freud's consider his final drive theory too speculative, or they feel it is *"uncanny" (unheimlich),* if the pleasure principle is subordinated to the death-drive. (Heenen-Wolff 2003, 61).

---

6   Cf. also Laplanche and Pontalis 1972, 495; A. Green 2005 a), 281.

However, the notion "uncanny" will quickly lead us to unconscious material, as Freud elaborated in his essay about "Das Unheimliche". Further thoughts to this topic regarding psychoanalysts were recently presented by Michael Parsons (2010, unpublished paper, 4-7). Parsons showed how analysts adopt a theoretical position that suits their character structure better than others and how they might feel destabilised by unusual ways of thinking, with which they are not "at home", this means, also etymologically, which are "un-heim-lich" for them. In "un-heim-lich" the prefix un- negates Heim = home, thus meaning "not at home". This is especially true for issues outside our familiar range of experience. But for analysts it is not enough "to analyse well on one's psychic home ground", they have to "play well away from home too" (Parsons).

Bettina Reiter was certainly right to call the theory of the death-drive an effort to grasp somehow the uncanny of the biological side of life psychologically and to verbalize the narcissistic injury, that we are in the history of genera – as individuals – a quantity to be neglected (Reiter 1996, 41).

Death, however, must be uncanny for everybody, or if it is not and if it is attractive with a perverse allure, it is a serious problem all the more, because then *Eros gets lost*.

II.

Missing fortunately any real own experience of the terror of dying we might now first turn to some "flashes of insight" (Winnicott) of a poet of Copenhagen: Hans Christian ANDERSEN. He is famous for his fairy tales, but he wrote also six novels. In one of them, an autobiographical novel entitled "To be or not to be", first published in 1857, ["At vaere ellere ikke vaerre"] he describes the lonely death of the main character Niels Bryde, who participated as medical doctor in the war between Denmark and Germany and died on the battlefield (189 ff.):

Niels is shocked by the sudden sting in his chest, he loses his eyesight, his bonds to the world are loosening, he feels to be in a transitional state, becoming a thing; something superior in him reinforces him for a moment. Suddenly he has the fearful imagination that his eyes will be penetrated by the enemy's bayonet. His external perceptions are passing into chaos, and a horrible fear of annihilation he had never felt before overwhelms him. There is nothing but pain, which will culminate in his extinction. He throws himself into the abyss of nothingness, and dying he thinks: 'Over! That is my life …. that is life … an eternal cycle'. Not far from him a horse is dying. And his dog comes and sits whining close to his head.

In 2003, Franco De Masi wrote "Making death thinkable." This text about "the theme of death, whose unrelenting harshness arouses anxieties akin to a catastrophic trauma" (preface), was awarded with the first Gradiva Price, in Lavarone, where Freud had written his Gradiva paper.

De Masi emphasizes the polarities[7]:

- Freud left us with two incompatible ways of understanding the death drive[8]: a) as a catastrophic occurrence and b) as a quiet return to a Nirvana state.
- Our "natural tendency to *deny death"* (p. 37) is opposed to our human capacity to *discern what we do not know and what we do know*.
- We are hardly aware of our own death, but of other people's death.
- We accept the biological fact of our mortality, and this knowledge results in the idea of immortality of the soul, pervading "both the individual and the collective imaginary. The very notion of immortality comes from the awareness of our mortality. Without one, there would not be the other" (p. 36).
- De Masi hints at the exuberance of death present in our civilisation opposed to a lack of digesting it: everyday the media inform us about "items concerning individual or collective deaths, murders or destruction carried out in every part of the world. What seems to have been lost is not so much an objective picture of death as an emotional awareness and a possibility of working it through" (p. 38).
- However, we need that awareness of death, of nothingness, in order to free ourselves from illusions, to accept death as our immanent destiny and to achieve a higher level of autonomy and authenticity (p. 68).We are reminded of Freud's modification of an old Latin proverb: si vis vitam, para mortem (if you want to be alive, get ready for death) (p. 132).

De Masi provokes a lot of thoughts:

He points at the fact that our concepts owe their origin to comparisons. This is a thought Freud himself elaborated in "The antithetical meaning of primal words" (1909). For instance we should not be able to distinguish light from dark, if it were always light. Only later on two sides of an antithesis were separated and hence it could be thought of one without conscious comparison with the other. Freud wrote that it was a publication of the philologist Karl Abel, published in 1884, that helped him finally to understand the dream-work's singular tendency to disregard negation and to employ the same means of representation for expressing contraries. Abel described the peculiarity in the oldest languages that a fair number of words have two meanings, one of which is the exact oppo-

---

[7] There might be a possibility to integrate these polarities by taking into account different time perspectives and wishful attempts at recovery.

[8] One might wonder how death and drive – utmost extremes – can come together in one German word: "Todestrieb" (Wolfgang Lassmann, personal communication, 4.3.2011).

site of the other. If we try to understand the unthinkable event of death, we are recurring to comparisons.

In a discussion of Simo Salonen's paper given in Delphi "The Body and the Sense of Reality" I dealt with the antithetical meaning of primal words, focusing on three aspects: on Salonen's remark that "body" refers to a living as well as to a dead person; on Freud's "Antithetical meaning of primal words" and on the polarity of life and lifelessness, resulting in the need of a limited confidence in body, life and nature. "Maybe the original screening of a continuum and the comparison of extremes still provides a better orientation and therefore greater security" (Zwettler-Otte 2006, 42).

Regarding De Masi's hint at the exuberance of death present in our civilization we might be reminded of the exuberance of snakes on Medusa's head after the shock of decapitation=castration, cf. Freud: Medusa's Head. (Zwettler-Otte 2011, chapter 7.2). Exuberance might be an alarm signal pointing at a shock and a difficulty in working it out.

The need of the acceptance of death we find already in the fairy tale of the brothers Grimm: it is entitled "Gevatter Tod". The moral drawn of this fairy tale is that our influence on fate and our achievements are great, as long as we respect the laws of nature and death. As soon as we try to deny them due to our wishful thinking and cheat, we fail: the fairy tale is about the failure of a successful medical doctor. He had once got a special gift by the Death: he had the capacity to see the Death near the feet of a patient, who had to die, but near the head, if the patient could be saved by a special herb. Once the doctor should cure the beautiful daughter of the king, but Death appeared at her feet. The doctor, incapable to accept this message, ignored the warning and gave her the medicine – and had therefore to die himself.

III.

Additionally to the general human difficulties to face death and transience, there are *very special problems that we have as psychoanalysts:*

1. *The acknowledgement of our limitations*: we are "indeed, unable to provide adequate answers to a real terror", trying often "to reduce the real fear of death to a personal problem", using theory defensively (De Masi, 2003, 66). Pathologizing the fear of death we are denying its traumatic and catastrophic impact on all human beings, including psychoanalysts. De Masi reminds us of personal experiences during medical examinations, whenever we come in contact with warning signals of our bodies, and of the relief we feel, when it turns out to be "just a false alarm" (66). Even Freud seems to imply that (un-

conscious) castration anxiety causes fear of death, and Melanie Klein suggests to work through persecutory anxiety to get liberated from the terror of dying. "Both of them appear to set aside the real anxiety and think that it may be possible to achieve Socrates' calm posture vis-à-vis death" (p. 66-68). Anyway, our bankruptcy regarding real catastrophes is nothing new. It is simply the capitulation we have to make confronted with reality. Nature and unstoppable biological forces silently at work in every living being belong to reality. And our undeletable death anxiety makes sense: it is a warning signal, which is biologically useful; it is part of ourselves and a reality that we cannot eliminate. De Masi opens one chapter with a motto of Luis Borges, who tries to make us feel that we are actively part of the untameable nature: *"Time is the substance I am made of (...). Time is a river that carries me away, but I am that river; it is a tiger that tears me to pieces, but I am that tiger; it is a fire that devours me, but I am that fire."* (Jorge Luis Borges, quoted in De Masi, 34)

2. Thus being reminded of our limits we might control, whether in becoming psychoanalysts – *experts of the unconscious* – *a secret hope has eventually returned that now we will become masters in our own house.* Such arrogance would be a step back, forgetting about the reality principle and the concept of the negativity from which the unconscious is constituted. If this disappointment not to be master in our own house is repressed, it might have found another outlet, for instance in a "fear of breakdown" of psychoanalysis, thus imagining a 'crisis' and a destruction of our 'unreliable' science. The source of this fantasy would be unconscious rage and fear.

3. While both acknowledgements of our limitations are narcissistic problems, we might also come in *conflict with our superego* and incline to compensate also for other specific problems like the difference between psychoanalytic knowledge and positive sciences, or the uncertainties of psychoanalytic cure:

   a) *First the scientific department of the superego,* which sometimes is an envious one (cf. Britton 2003, 125 ff*.):* Today it seems difficult for psychoanalysts to prove them worth, when bureaucratic protocols are requested, "while our practice is portrait-painting", as Gregorio Kohon said in his paper given at the EPF-Conference in London 2010.

   This metaphor is pointing to the same way, which Peter Passett from Swiss suggests: we should be proud of the specific strength of psychoanalysis: the metaphoric way of thinking and fantasying, which often is not acknowledged in sciences, banished to art, religion and pseudo-science. This *visionary capacity of thinking* belonged in former times to the rhetoric sciences. Psychoanalysis has the power to bring this *"forgotten thinking, the drive-base of thinking",* which is based on the binding, linking capac-

ity of Eros, back into the realm of scientific knowledge, offering to other disciplines the chance to look at the foundation for an integration of all knowledge (Passett 1992, 138ff).

Only if we ourselves also forget about the power of fantasy with its flash-like comprehension of similarities (and of opposite poles, I would like to add), we too are stepping back. It would be another lost step to neglect this and instead to take on the mask of a rational positive science, which does not suit us and includes the seduction to search for a final and certain rest, a wish, which belongs to the death drive (Passett 1992, 141).

Regarding contacts to other scientific disciplines there is a range from justified efforts to build bridges to hopeless and exhausting, self-destructive subordinations.

There were attempts from the very beginnings to secure academic recognition for psychoanalysis. For instance Eduard Hitschmann, a distinguished internal specialist, the Freud's sometime family doctor and a member of the Wednesday Society, to which his friend Paul Federn had introduced him, supported this idea skilfully and well organized. Nevertheless, the fundamental difference to positive sciences caused always problems. Freud ultimately kept some distance from Hitschmann, though he valued his commitment and loyalty highly (Zwettler-Otte, 2006). It is another example that shows the similarities between the early reception of psychoanalysis and our situation nowadays.

b) There can also be struggles with the superego-demands represented by intellectual and political authorities who have to decide about public money for psychotherapy (*economical department*). These problems result in the clinical practitioner's challenge which "will inevitably remain open and unresolved: the question of the uncertainty of the psychoanalytic cure" (Kohon 1999, 150).

4. One of the greatest fears, however, might be that *we cannot even rely on the pleasure-principle*, because it can change the ends and – as Freud pointed out – "serve the death instincts" (1920, SE 18, 63). Thus we will sometimes meet the deep bond between pleasure and annihilation, extinguishing any desire and calming any aggressive or sexual wish (Heenen-Wolff, 2003, 65, 67). This *silent reversal* is not only a danger common to all human beings, but also one that threatens to kill our work with patients who suffer from masochism, guilt, negative therapeutic reaction or other manifestations of the "work of the negative" (Green 1999).

5. Finally we have to consider once more, *how closely the analyst's personality and his anxieties and methods are intermingled.* An example of this became a matter of concern among the analysts, when serious boundary violations of

Winnicott's most prominent former candidate Masud Khan became public due to the article "Saving Masud Khan" by his former patient Wynne Godley. (A.-M. Sandler 2007). The following discussions about Khan's transgressions led A. Green (2005, 35 ff.) – with respect and regret – to the conclusion, that Winnicott "was blind to that part of psychoanalytic theory that was too close to his own pathology (being too nice, or being devilish)", that he did not recognize Khan's disguised way of castrating the father, stealing and destroying the father's penis because of envy." Winnicott did not take into consideration this aspect of Freudian theory, Khan's "provocations were to prove fruitless, since no father figure emerged and the 'holding' relationship did not have the capacity to overcome Khan's psychopathic behaviours" (Green 2005, 35), which resulted in serious ethical and technical problems, when he worked with his patients. Khan's destructiveness apparently could not become worked through sufficiently in his analysis with Winnicott. Khan became abandoned and left alone to struggle with his own self-destructive impulses. Regarding Winnicott, his analyst, it will not take us by surprise, that he rejected Freud's death drive theory as "false theory" (Winnicott, Human nature, 1991, 132 f.).

6. All these difficulties remind us of Freud's advice, that an analyst should "periodically – at intervals of five years or so – submit himself to analysis once more, without feeling ashamed of taking this step" (1937, Analysis terminable…SE 23, 243) *This advise is perhaps taken more often than we know, but perhaps also less often than necessary.* Green's supports Freud's advice suggesting a kind of periodical "military service for a few weeks" in "Time in Psychoanalysis" (Green, 2002, 46).

7. The death drive concept confronts us probably more than any other concept with *our need for the others.* "When we face death … we can only find solace in collective, rather than individual reparation" and De Masi explains: "Reparation consists in the arduous journey of many individual selves who leave themselves in other selves that will follow. (… It) can only be achieved through the projection of our past into the future, in the future of the others" (De Masi 2003, 125). This is a very difficult task, last, not least because our psychoanalytic societies usually are not experienced as *"facilitating environments"* by many individual members.

IV.

I conclude my paper with the case of a woman – I call her Eve – who again and again occurred to me, while I was thinking of our Panel. I suppose this was due to her secret involvement of death in her life, an unconscious effort to escape overwhelming pain, guilt and fear by deadening all wishes, adapting perfectly and enjoying nothing but hidden destructive triumphs.

Eve was 54, when she came for analysis; recommended by the analyst of her partner, who seemed to urge her to this step. Nevertheless, in the mood of "now-or-never" she insisted that she wanted to try to become now finally a "real woman", otherwise she feared to lose her friend, who recently had betrayed her for the first time. Actually, her appearance was that of a colourless little mouse, there could not be a greater distance to a seductive vamp.

A week after we had started analysis, she got the diagnosis "breast cancer". But unwavering in her wish for an analysis she suggested discussing the necessary interruptions during her stays in hospital. Soon it turned out that – as frightening as this "new attack against her femininity" was – *this* did not become the greatest challenge for our work. She managed all medical examinations, the operation and the following treatment apparently without great anxieties and without missing more sessions than absolutely necessary and behaved totally "reasonably" – a "virtue" she was praised for since childhood, as she told me.

Whenever I intended to question her emotionless attitude, she quickly tried to bring me back to her main issue: "how to become a real woman". She complained about her incapacity to devote herself to sexual intercourse with her partner, whom she loved tenderly. I saw myself excluded from her inner world. and tried to show her that in analysis, too, she avoided devotion to her feelings. Instead, Eve offered two bad solutions for me: I would either be as passive and impotent as her depressive mother, or intrusive in a sadistic way. Similar she lived in a symbiosis with her friend, but rejected his sexual approach as "intrusion" and enjoyed unconsciously and sado-masochistically castrating him. Eve listened, but was more interested in reconstructions[9] of her early years as a single child, feeling to be extremely close to her father. Looking back allowed her to see some dependence that in presence she had to disavow totally, defending violently a pseudo-independence, which was also regarding her transference her main unconscious omnipotent and narcissistic defensive position (Krejci 2011, 22) and forced her into an anti-oedipal fortress.

Once she came confused: "There was just such an unpleasant moment. By mistake I pressed in the lift the button to the 3rd floor, to your flat, not the 2nd, to your office!" She could not bear her wish to enter my privacy and denied to have

---

9   Junkers G. pointed at the difference between authors emphasizing the necessity of reconstructions and those stressing the need of working through the depressive position (Xii). I am convinced that both is equally necessary, the link to the past *and* the capacity of mourning. For my patient reconstructions were easier and quicker available due to her rationalising defence.

any desire to transgress professional boundaries. In her professional life as a teacher she, too, had a kind, but strongly restricted relationship to her pupils, and she assumed it would be the same with me. She defended violently her pseudo-independence, which allowed her also only a half-hearted use of analysis and made her control it by concentrating on her main issue, her obvious search for sexuality she did not miss at all. All wishes, all fears, all her libidinal desires and all her hate were suffocated in the bud and covered by a perfect adaptation. In one session she discovered: "Today I am dressed in green fitting totally to the couch". I interpreted that her mimicry was indeed – not only today – a perfect way of hiding; I was thinking of mimosis as a kind of defence (prior to primary identification), which D.-W. Eickhoff recently described as a beginning, but somehow delayed death (Eickhoff 2011, 68 f.).

Once – it was after a short break I had made – she dreamed that she was in a cold room, her dement mother had opened the window and smashed a valuable lamp. Hesitating she recognized her anger that I (represented by a dement mother) had left her alone in the cold. The dark, but also exciting atmosphere she described reminded me of a sentence by Henry Moore, referring to his nocturnal loneliness in Stonehenge: "*I was alone and tremendously impressed. (Moonlight, as you know, enlarges everything, and the mysterious depths and distances made it seem enormous.)" (Henry Moore, 1983, 117)*. Eve was reluctant to accept that she was hiding behind the role of "a shy, reasonable and tender little girl" very hateful and destructive feelings, which she projected onto me, full of fear of my revenge. I could not renounce using her narcissism as a slide and said, that sometimes it needs "courage to be afraid" and that there might be "dignity" in fear and even in tears of pain (Bolognini 2011, 185 ff.).

Her aggressive attacks against her (and my) femininity became more and more evident. She felt to be a hollow box in comparison to men. Her obvious fight for being a "real woman" had a heavy counterweight in her male identification, recently illustrated by a dream, in which she was lying in the desert, a lynx softly resting on her. Her associations showed that she felt to be both, the woman and the male lynx; if the lynx would use his claws, she might get hurt seriously. It seems, we have now progressed to a hysterical stage: Eve oscillates regarding the question: is she "a woman or a man.? Whom does she choose, mother or father?"… "In the end, the divalence of the hysteric only reveals the persistence in feminine sexuality of the uncertainty of desire" (Kohon 1999, 21-23).

In Eve's mind it was too dangerous to have desires and to devote oneself to somebody.

It occurred to her that once her father had slapped her unjustified, because he thought wrongly she had hidden his shoes. Some time later he lost his arm due to a current-accident. She felt desperately guilty, as if she had made him lose his arm as a punishment.

Her cancer she compared now with Camus' 'The Plague', seeing it as a misfortune without warning, forcing her to a permanent struggle, otherwise there would be left nothing but desperation. She came to see now, how she had over large periods withdrawn into a bucolic world, banishing and denying all her rage and despair and all her wishes, too. It was the only retreat, where she could renounce omnipotent control and independence.

When she felt depressed extending her hopeless feelings to the idea that I too would abandon all hope, I felt in my counter-transference the wish for compensation and for making stronger efforts than she did. She had delegated her wishes to others (her partner, or to me) in order to get rid of conflicts. For herself wishes were followed by catastrophes. However, her capacity to mourn (the lost time and her childlessness) and to feel mental pain as well as wishes increased a lot. Ending analysis is not yet near, but she raised this issue already, recognizing that it is too early. Sometimes she is stepping back to sado-masochistic complaints: *the seductive charm of what is impossible seems to be as great as the seductive charm of what is forbidden.* Even her appreciation of analysis is dubious, when she says that she now enjoys everything, also her relationship to her partner, so much more, "perhaps not although, but because it is too late …"

This case shows many *clinical phenomena* that we can understand using the concept of the death drive: from the *inaccessible real fear of death* (at the beginning of analysis due to the diagnosis of cancer) to the silent manifestations:

Some of them looked like virtues, for instance her reasonable behaviour, hiding her perverse satisfaction in suffering, or her economy, hiding her masochistic stinginess. One can see the patient's *destruction of the self:* her incapacity of investing herself as a woman (combined with envy of "real women"), her evacuation of sexual desire and her suffocation of own thoughts, own wishes, of own creativity and of feelings regarding her body and her needs, all these characteristics proved the work of the negative.

The disobjectalisation became evident in the tormenting quality of her relationship with her partner, based on an unconscious identification with her depressive mother and her father's condemnation of any dependence. It could also be experienced by both of us regarding the lack of resonance in the transference situation, her elimination of my significance for her, her pseudo-independence and her retreat in an anti-oedipal fortress.

The patient's conscious wish to become a "real woman" was connected with a vague awareness that something was seriously wrong; it was an attempt at recovery, but too weak to succeed without help: a powerless wish, floating on the surface like a water-lily, cut off from its rootstock. Psychoanalysis seems to be able to connect her again with life.

In formulating some of our anxieties and concerns as precisely as possible, as Peter Wegner suggested (2011, 3), we might feel encouraged to continue our vacillating rhythm of conquering psychoanalytic knowledge, "wavering between moments of lucidity and new confusions in order to be capable of sometimes leaving the usual ways of theory, since every arrival on this journey includes the danger of getting stuck and lifeless" (Gross R. 2009, 90.). And Rainer Gross referred to Samuel Beckett[10], who wrote an encouraging sentence; which has to do with losing steps:

"Ever tried. Ever failed. No matter. Try again. Fail again. Fail better."

References

Andersen, H.C. (1857 <2005>): Sein oder nicht sein. Frankfurt am Main: Fischer Tb

Bolognini, St. (2011): Secret Passages. The Theory and Technique of Interpsychic Relations. London: Routledge

Britton, R. (2003): Sex, Death, and the Superego. London: Karnac

Danckwardt, J. F. (2011): Die Verleugnung des Todestriebs. In: Jahrbuch der Psychoanalyse, 62, 137-163

De Masi, F. (2004): Making death thinkable. UK: Free Association Books

Eickhoff, F. W. (2011): Primäre Identifizierung: Plädoyer für ein umstrittenes Konzept. In: Psyche, 65 Jg./1

Fliess, R. (1956): Erogeneity and Libido. Some Addenda. N.Y.: Int. Uni. Press

Freud, S. (1919): The Uncanny. SE 17

Freud, S. (1920): Beyond the Pleasure principle, SE 18

Freud, S. (1922): Medusa's Head, SE 18

Freud, S. (1937): Analysis Terminable and Interminable, SE 23

Green, A. (1999): The work of the Negative. London: Free Association Books

Green, A. (2005 a): Key ideas for a contemporary Psychoanalysis. East Sussex: Routledge

Green, A. (2005 b): Play and reflection in Donald Winnicott's Writings. London: Karnac

Gross, R. (2009): Die Frustration durch Nicht-Wissen aushalten. Zur emotionalen Erfahrung des Lesens von Bion-Texten. In: Zeitschrift für Psychoanalytische Theorie und Praxis; 24. Jg., Heft 1

---

10 Beckett was Bion's patient as a young man.

Heenen-Wolff, S. (2003): Freuds Konzept des Todestriebs – welcher Nutzen für den psychoanalytischen Alltag? In: Zeitschrift für Psychoanalytische Theorie und Praxis; 18. Jg., Heft 1

Junkers, G. (Ed.) (2006): Is it too late? Key papers on psychoanalysis and ageing. London: Karnac

Kohon, G. (1999): No lost certainties to be recovered. London: Karnac

Kohon, G. (2010): Love in transference – Primary identification and the maternal imago. Paper given at the EPF-Conference in London 2010. (Italian translation: Amore nel transfert. Identificatione primaria e imago materna. In: Psicoanalisi, Vol. 14, Numero 2, Iuglio-dicembre

Krejci, E. (2011): Freuds "Ichspaltung im Abwehrvorgang und die Erweiterung des Neurosenmodells". In: Psyche, 65 Jg./1

Laplanche, J., Pontalis, J.-B. (1972): Das Vokabular der Psychoanalyse: Frankfurt am Main: Suhrkamp

Moore, H. (1983): Ausstellungskatalog ‚Henry Moore in Wien', Wien: Habarta Kunsthandel & Verlag

Parsons, M. (2010): Death and Primal scene (including Orpheus and the Uncanny) (not yet published)

Passet, P. (1992): Ein Seher. Das Negative im Auge: Mit dem Tod gegenden Tod. In: Kuster M.: Entfernte Wahrheit. Von der Endlichkeit der Psychoanalyse. Tübingen: edition diskord

Reiter, B. (1996): Dunkel ist das Leben, ist der Tod. Zu Freud's Todestriebtheorie. In: Zeitschrift Für psycho-analytische Theorie und Praxis. Jg. XI, 1

Quinodoz, J.-M. (2005): Reading Freud: A chronological exploration of Freud's writings. USA and Canada: Routledge

Sandler, A.-M. (2007): Reaktionen der psychoanalytischen Institutionen auf Grenzverletzungen – Masud Khan und Winnicott. In: Zwettler-Otte S.: Entgleisungen in der Psychoanalyse.

Salonen, S. (2006): The body and the sense of reality. In: Beyond the Mind-Body-Dualism: Psychoanalysis and the Human Body. Ed.: Evy Zacharacopoulou. Athens. Elsevier

Wegner, P. (2011): Anxiety and Method in Psychoanalysis. Program to the EPF-Conference Copenhagen

Winnicott, D.W. (1991): Human Nature. London: Free Association Books

Zwettler-Otte, S. (2005): From Freud's "Splendid Isolation" to our "Crisis" today – An Attempt to interpret Internal Conflicts Past and Present, EPF-Bulletin 59

Zwettler-Otte, S. (2006): The body and the sense of reality – Discussion of Simo Salonen's paper. In: Beyond the Mind-Body-Dualism: Psychoanalysis and the Human Body. Ed.: Evy Zacharacopoulou. Athens. Elsevier

Zwettler-Otte, S. (2006): Freud and the Media: The Reception of Psychoanalysis in Viennese Medical Journals 1895-1938. Frankfurt-Berlin-Wien: Peter Lang Internationaler Verlag der Wissenschaften
Zwettler-Otte, S. (2007): Entgleisungen in der Psychoanalyse. Berufsethische Probleme. Göttingen: Vandenhoeck & Ruprecht
Zwettler-Otte, S. (Ed.) (2009): „… durch 1000 Kanäle und Poren. Frankfurt-Berlin-Wien. Peter Lang Internationaler Verlag der Wissenschaften.

Sketches in the Patient's Magic Drawing Book[11]

I.

In my beginning is my end.
(T.S. Eliot 1974, 196)

When an analysis comes to an end, there is sometimes an excited movement: the patient is looking anxiously forward and sadly backward, staggering between both directions. Recalling the beginning of the treatment an initial secret project can be detected, a hidden unconscious plan the patient had in his mind to let the psychoanalysis either succeed or fail. This is a limited aspect, which of course can hardly be separated from the whole experience shared by the potential patient and the psychoanalyst during the total situation of the initial interview. Nevertheless, it might be worthwhile to focus on this basic attitude of the ongoing analysand regarding his unconscious intention to start a hopeful or a hopeless enterprise.

Seemingly unimportant details of the start can reveal a deep meaning that was always there but can be understood only after the long and hard work of analysis, similar to children's magic drawing pages, which reveal a picture only after a lot of scribbling on the seemingly empty pages.

This initially unconscious draft emerges – according to my experience – often again at the end of an analysis. It turns up as a mixture of memories concerning the expectations at the beginning of the treatment and of condensations worked out "nachträglich" at the end of the analysis. Looking back to the beginning of their analysis some patients are well aware that it is their need to mourn the ending of the analysis, which forces their associations to go back to the be-

---

11 This paper was presented at the EPF-Conference 2012 in Paris in a Panel with Jordi Sala (Spain) and John Boots (Australia).

ginning.[12] This natural and spontaneous movement of the psychoanalytic process reminds of Freud's observation that analysis like the "noble art of chess" allows for a detailed systematic demonstration only regarding the opening and the final games, "whilst the overwhelming variety of games after the opening resists such a demonstration." (Freud 1913, SE 12, 123) I'll present a case and then try to elaborate some of the constellations of the initial phase, which I found in several analyses re-emerging during the final phase. *Thus, I'll deal with the initial interview, seen from the end of the analytic treatment.*

"It has already all been there in our very first meeting" a female, 34 years old patient, whom I'll call here Susan, said in one of her last sessions. She was surprised and repeated:

"It was all there, but I could not see it."

She was thinking of her initial interview, to which she came a bit late, like today – this was worth mentioning, because all the years of her analysis she never had been late again, and now it has happened once more. It reminded her of her *initial disorientation*, which had caused her delay, when she came to her first appointment a few minutes late. She had lost her way, mixing up the streets. It reflected her emotional confusion, which to her surprise turned out to be stronger than her careful calculation of the new way and the time needed to come to my office. Only *after* the first interview she felt a *tremendous fear*: What would have happened to her, if I would not have agreed to see her once more and finally, after a second session, if I would not have been ready to take her into analysis? On the surface she had felt sovereign, giving a psychoanalytic enterprise "just one more try" after some failures with psychotherapies and planning to give it up finally, if there would arise any difficulty in our first appointment. But when she had left me after the 2nd interview with clear arrangements put down in her agenda, she thought of the ballade about the "Reiter und der Bodensee" (The Rider and the Bodensea). This poem by Gustav Schwab is about a man, who collapsed dead by shock, when he learned that he was not about to do, but had just done the dangerous ride over a frozen sea. Suddenly Susan became aware, that she had been terribly afraid I might reject her and she might get more and more lost in a lonely battle against her hidden madness. Later on we could see also the other side of her fear: there was also some secret hope that she could escape and that there would be a chance of avoiding to enter into the psychoanalytic relationship with me. As Thomas Ogden wrote "Everything in the first

---

12 Together with the need for mourning often also a tendency comes up to integrate the whole psychoanalytic experience as a "Gestalt" and to understand it in a more realistic way. Now the Secondary Process is on advance, opposed to the beginning, which often gives way to the pressing Primary Process.

hours can be heard in the light of an unconscious warning to the analyst" (Ogden 2011, 180), and we might add: 'and to the patient him- or herself'.

Fear and disorientation, the dominant feelings at the start of Susan's analysis, had returned now in the last year of her analysis. She recognized both feelings, although they differed decisively in degree and quality: the fear was no longer unconscious, but ready for working through, and her disorientation was looking for a new orientation. She was afraid whether she would continue to manage her life well enough, when she had left me. She was worried whether I would allow her to see me again, if she would need or simply wish it. Her initial concern I might reject her reappeared. She had doubts whether her new stability was strong enough or was just a fake. And although she was quite satisfied now with her private life and her professional carrier, she felt that any change could destabilize her once more and she might lose orientation again.

Nevertheless, fear and insecurity decreased soon, when we discovered her *wish* to go back to the start in order not to part with me. When we grasped also her disappointment that I did not keep her back, she confessed that she also wanted to punish me for this and to show me, that "nothing at all has changed", she was still anxious and uncertain.

"Both terrible feelings of fear and confusion were there also in our very first meeting, but I could not even see it", Susan said, and this simple statement reminded her of *the magic drawing books of her childhood*: there were only white pages, but when the child scribbled and scrawled over the seemingly empty pages, a picture appeared. Susan said: "In the kindergarten I liked to scribble in a magic drawing book; especially, when I later on learned to look more closely on the white sheet of paper and got a feeble glimpse, what kind of picture might come out, if I scribbled long enough." This was – I felt – quite an impressive metaphor for the first encounter of a patient with an analyst, who can get just a faint idea of what the analytic relationship will be like, if they work long and intensively enough together. Of course, analysis takes much longer than a scribbling game. Freud wrote about analysis in "The Question of Lay Analysis":

> *"It would be magic, if it worked rather quicker. An essential attribute of a magician is speed – one might say suddenness – of success. But analytic treatments take months and even years: magic that is so slow loses its miraculous character."*
>
> (Freud S. 1926, p. 187)

Given the fact that due to an enlarged spectrum of indications and higher demands nowadays analyses take much more time than Freud had in mind, we have to face that today *being an analyst means to be a rather slow magician*.

Anyway, Susan herself had needed her time to diagnose that she needed help. But after the first interview she managed in spite of her demanding professional tasks rather easily to organize time for her analysis. She quickly developed a strong transference and imagined already during the first sessions, as soon as she used the couch that *she might never become able to get up again*. This was a last warning to me and to herself that now not her capacity for rational control, but something else would take over and explode. And it did explode. Becoming overwhelmed by her regressive desires and her tyrannical fears there were moments where we both had doubts whether she could bear a psychoanalytic process or whether she would break down. However, these concerns remained somehow without internal echo. She strictly stuck to our arrangements; her ability to work was hardly infected and she did not withdraw too much from external reality, whilst her whole drama developed *in* analysis. This encouraged me and enabled her to say in a short break of the internal stormy weather: "Already when I left you after our first appointment there was – in spite of my terrible confusion and my shock that I had been late and thus unreliable – a *tremendous relief*. It was as if I could clearly state that I had now made an important step into the right direction – wherever this direction would lead." Her readiness to take her analysis serious seemed to contain both: her need and longing for that miraculous kind of relationship with me, and her unconscious intention to place pressure upon me and to make me "conform to an unconsciously wished-for role", as A-M. and J. Sandler described it (J., Sandler A.-M. 1998, 47 ff.). While she did everything to see me, she felt that I was the one who failed to be always there for her and thus in her view rejected her. *I* tried to show her in which way she wished to manipulate me and that she was "not only the victim of [her] symptoms, but also the director of the history of [her] suffering", as Peter Wegner put it (Wegner 2011, p. 232). The role she tried to force on me was that of a desperately desired object that would refuse her. In her reliability was from the very beginning stubbornness and aggression, but also an impressive strength. Already in our first meeting she came running like a haunted victim, being just about 3 or 4 minutes late, but she did calm down and give a clear description of her personal situation.

She imposed on me the role of a distracted and rejecting mother, and in my counter-transference I felt either helpless and guilty as she did, or in need to defend myself that I tried to stick to an analytic attitude. "Wavering between the patient's inner reality and simultaneously my own reality testing" (Amati-Mehler 2011, p. 109), was quite confusing and exhausting. Anyway, I recognized that I had to respond to, but not to take her role-offer. In a typical constellation of our intrapsychic role-relationship I interpreted her unconscious search for masochistic suffering. Susan became furious that I addressed her secret intention to become disappointed and rejected and that I allocated to her the active role of the director of a drama. However, soon she started to realize that the analyst's work was a fight against her hidden project by shedding light upon it. I had somehow become the producer who refused to give the director of her tragedy further economical support; thus the game was over.

Susan had not been conscious of her tremendous fear of entering into a new relationship, a psychoanalytic relationship with me. She had seen me just once, when I gave a public paper about *"The Melody of Separation – a psychoanalytic study on separation-anxiety"*. She was touched by my remark that looking young can be a pleasant psychosomatic symptom. She had not expected an analyst to say something she considered funny, and perhaps she felt that she herself looked according to her psycho-sexual development like a frightened girl, in contrast to her intellectual achievements. This very evening she had the idea of giving me a call to ask for a consultation. It took nearly two months until she did it. We can see that her approach to her analyst started quite a long time before the first interview[13].

The anxieties that had delayed her phone call increased tremendously on the day, when she finally was on the way to my office. On the conscious level there was nothing but hurry and excitement. On a deeper level she had a sense that our first meeting in my consulting room meant the initiation of a psychoanalytic process, which might turn her psychic reality upside down and might endanger her capacity to act in the external world skilfully controlling everything. This had been until now one of the few sources of protection she felt she had.

The conscious reason, why she came to me, was a very disappointing experience with a highly estimated colleague, who rejected to work with her, because he considered her not yet enough trained for a specific task. Susan knew that he was right, but she felt totally devaluated and rejected. She thought she needed just a few appointments with me to overcome this slight. However, she also told me that her depressed mood was not new. It had started long ago and had a lot to do with her history as a single child of a mother, who was so anxious that Susan felt she could hardly see her, and a father, whom she experienced close in the early years, but who often lost his temper and withdrew later on, so that Susan felt rejected.

In her first interview, Susan apologized for her short delay: she had just wanted to enter on the way to me the yards of a few houses in my surrounding. She did not know this district very well and liked the old buildings. They reminded her of the place where her father had worked, and she was especially interested to have a look inside of these buildings. Thinking of her father, who had died three years ago, had brought her – very untypically – into a nearly dreamlike state, and she had forgotten to look at her watch. *This short episode,*

---

13 We even could go back much further to find traces of her so-called 'interest' in psychoanalysis, meaning that she felt touched by some psychoanalytic thoughts she happened to hear or read.

which she reported in a hectic way as an unimportant minor matter, was later on in her analysis filled with important meanings, to which I'll return. In our first meeting she could already recognize that she might have hesitated a bit to come, and that her strange detours into the yards of attractive buildings had caused a wished-for delay of our real meeting. Ringing at my door she was afraid I might send her home again immediately for being late- a projection of her unconscious resistance against the analytic enterprise. To forget about the time had increased her anxiety, because it proved to her that she had lost her perfect functioning already before she had done the first step into my office. During the two months before she made an appointment with me she had been terribly concerned *how any conversation with an analyst, who was a stranger to her, might work*: she could not imagine allowing so much intimacy in the context of a formal meeting. Maybe I would fix her in a much too long analysis, which also would endanger her financial independence. During the first interview, she gave me a hint that she could not afford to buy a sailing boat she would like very much. Later on she revealed that she had said this to let me know that she was not rich and I should not ask for a high fee.

I try to summarize some main points of her first interview:

- On her way to me Susan had unusually lost control and had drifted away in memories and daydreams connected with her father. She was conscious of her excitement and pressure, but not of her fear.
- Her fear, which we addressed in the first session only as 'a feeling of uneasiness' had several sources:
  - She felt that she lost her balance: primary *process was on advance.*
  - Before unfolding the transference she was still aware that I was a stranger to her. She thought about the contradiction of intimacy and formality. Such clear and realistic thoughts had to get slowly drowned in the transference.
  - Being afraid of her own demanding and symbiotic wishes, which she projected on me, she warned me – and herself – with an air of growing resignation.
- In spite of this emotional storm (Bion 1987) and the percussions of her equilibrium she left me after the first session with a feeling of a great relief and of moving into the right direction.

II.

> In my end is my beginning.
> (T.S. Eliot, 1974, 204)

In the last year, as soon as ending had become the main issue, the initial interview and the first sessions were repeatedly moving into the foreground. It was mainly her fear and her uncertainty, which led her back to the start. Once when a dream seemed to be full of hints regarding the end of our work, she was shocked and full of separation anxiety, and the first line of a poem by Hermann Hesse occurred to her: "Alle Tode bin ich schon gestorben – I have died already all deaths". The last verse of this poem – she recalled – spoke about a trembling bow trying to bend[14] both poles of life, birth and death, together. Susan was tortured by her desire to go back to the beginning in order to prolong the treatment, which had – in spite of all ups and downs – provided for her a certain feeling of being protected and cared for. How could she come to be ready to leave this certain path? Anyway, staying would not only mean to act against her natural impulse to progress, but also to damage my help, and this was incompatible with her feeling of gratitude. Occasionally she described very clearly, how she felt enriched by the "personal knowledge" that had grown by those interpretations she had "tried out and tested" in diverse situations and thus had become her own (Kohon 2007, 204). Susan's effort to create 'infinity' by going back to the beginning and to form an endless circle had to fail.

It became more and more evident that it was this conflict, which seemed unbearable to her: the conflict between the wish to have a happy end for this good experience of analysis, and her wish to stay with me forever.

It was fascinating for both of us, when she once again looked back to her first interview and found suddenly some meaning in her detour through the yards, which had caused her short delay. Entering private houses near to my house was in her fantasy connected with exploring internal spaces, and finally she thought of her mother's womb: from there after her own birth, only a dead baby had come out, when Susan was 8 years old. She had felt so guilty about her incapac-

---

14 Oh zitternd gespannter Bogen, / wenn der Sehnsucht rasende Faust / beide Pole des Lebens / zueinander zu biegen verlangt! / Oft noch und oftmals wieder / wirst Du mich jagen von Tod zu Geburt / der **Gestaltungen** schmerzvolle Bahn, / der **Gestaltungen** herrliche Bahn." / (S I, p. 73).

Oh trembling flexed bow, / when the furious fist of desire / demands to bend both poles of life / together! / Often again and again / you will chase me from death to birth / the painful path of designings, / the magnificent path of designings.

ity to share her mother's despair and sadness. Beside her guilt feelings that she had had very ambivalent thoughts regarding a sibling, she felt also some hostility towards her mother, who had been unable to keep an embryo alive. Susan now turned more to her father at that time. However, this enlarged her guilt that she rejected her mourning mother. She remembered now that her mother had complained to her some years later that after the miscarriage the father had totally withdrawn from her and never had intercourse with her again in order to avoid in future such a catastrophe.

Susan somehow identified with her father regarding his sexual role. Entering private yards got now also the meaning that she was the intruder, penetrating an internal space. She did what her father should have done according to the desire of her mother. And suddenly she remembered how guilty she had felt that before calling me to arrange our first appointment she had to overcome her resistance against a female analyst. She would have preferred a man, but I was the only analyst whom she had at least once seen, and she did not want to ask anybody for further recommendations. She was afraid I might be as vulnerable as her mother and I might be also incapable of holding her, as her mother had not been able to hold at least the second baby. She herself had always felt dropped, when her mother was concerned with her anxieties regarding her health or some disagreements with her surroundings.

The concept of divalence, which Gregorio Kohon elaborated (Kohon 1984; 1999; 2007) helped a lot to understand now also Susan's permanent wavering between contradictory options, which finally had led us to her sexual disorientation. Kohon wrote: "I have put forward the idea that the subject is confronted, at a certain point of the Oedipal drama, with the choice between mother and father. This is a *hysterical stage*, a developmental moment characterized by what I called *divalence:* not being able to choose between mother and father as the primary sexual object" (Kohon 2007, p. 208).[15]

By getting lost in the yards Susan marked from the very beginning the moment, in which she became "caught up in her need to change object from mother to father – [She was] unable to make the necessary choice" (Kohon 1999, p. 18 f.). At the end of Susan's analysis we could understand that intruding into inner

---

15 I cannot go here into details concerning Susan's diagnosis, but I want to mention that she, too, like many patients, might have been diagnosed as a hysteric person at Freud's times, but was now diagnosed as Borderline, mainly because of the official diagnose-schema for insurances. Kohon pointed out clearly, that such a shift in diagnoses "is not the result of a change in the population of patients but a consequence of a change in the theory of psychoanalysis (Kohon 2007, 208)". Susan presented normally a great capacity for reality testing and was without doubt not psychotic; but she was not in the possession of a sense of identity, which a merely neurotic person would have had.

spaces symbolized her "phallic attachment to her mother". The yards were an impressive and very concrete symbolization of being half outside, half inside. Susan's sexual development itself represented her incapacity to make a choice: the penis of her father attracted her, but she could not leave her mother who had withheld from her attentive closeness. She had been highly confused to find only a female analyst, which meant to her to make a step back again. Nevertheless, that she felt touched and well enough understood in the first interview, gave her the feeling that she had done a step in the right direction. Actually, it was a progress, that she could *acknowledge* her hidden search for a mother, although it looked like a pure regression to her. It was like discovering the hook, on which she was hanging. Entering private spaces symbolized both: being a baby that crawled back in mother's womb, and being the phallic intruder. Susan's search for a holding mother had often interfered with her conscious wish to find a male partner. Her general extreme ambivalence[16] stemmed from her divalent position. This state Kohon described in the following way:

> *"always remaining in the middle, weaving constantly between one and the other, without getting close to either: stranded half-way, she postulates the impossible. She is half participating, half excluded. [...] She hopes that her frigidity will be her safeguard."*
>
> (Kohon 1999, p. 19 f.)

Susan's hobby was fashion. But also this had not helped her to feel as an attractive woman. Even when she – seldom enough – was satisfied with her look, she felt disguised: "she will pretend to be a woman, will put on the fancy dress proper to what she believes", but she does not feel to be a woman due to her phallic identification, Kohon wrote (Kohon 1999, 3). Associating to a dream she once had said that she would not have achieved anything in her profession, if she did not feel deeply inside as if she were a man.

It was as if her nearly manic activities served as a defence against her primary identification with her anxious mother, whom she believed to detest. There seemed to be in Susan the presence of a primary identification with a maternal imago that is experienced only in extreme terms. On the one hand, this imago epitomized an omnipotent, protective, powerful maternal figure she was desperately looking for. On the other hand, the same imago personified a vulnerable, helpless, ill and anxious figure. Susan's unconscious reminiscence of her strug-

---

16 Like for many psychic disturbances, also for divalence there are attractive professions, where oscillating between opposite poles is not disturbing, but seems to be a virtue. Susan, for instance, in a mood to identify with me and to approach to a psychotherapeutic work, thought of studying mediation. However, she dropped this idea in the last year of her analysis and decided to continue her carrier in her own profession.

gles with this primary imago of an absolute mother constituted the background, against which her object relationships developed (Kohon 2010). This primary imago, whose omnipotence cannot only easily collapse, but also become dangerous and devouring, reminds of the archaic mother represented as Sphinx (cf. Alain Gibeault and Stefano Bolognini in this volume).

"It was already all there in the first interview", Susan recognized embarrassed, "but I had not been able to see it", she added and thought once more of the magic drawing pages, which revealed their pictures only after a long scribbling. The first interview had provoked an emotional storm (Bion 1987), so did also the end of Susan's analysis. But although a storm was roaring around her, she now was standing rather calm in the middle, still a bit anxious and with an air of resignation. One day – it was in the last month of her analysis – she brought me a copy of a page of T. S. Eliot, because there she had found her "growing terror of nothing" expressed perfectly well, and she wanted me to read it.

> *"I said to my soul, be still, and wait without hope*
> *For hope would be hope for the wrong thing; wait without love*
> *For love would be love of the wrong thing; there is yet faith*
> *But the faith and the love and the hope are all in the waiting."*

(T.S. Eliot 1974, 200 f.)

This poem of T.S. Eliot contained also a hint at the poles of beginning and ending, speaking of "the agony of death and birth".

Susan had given up hope that she could imagine how she would experience the time after we would have stopped to meet nearly every day. What would happen to her strong feelings, which she knew that psychoanalytic theory named transference? Would she be able to bear the loss? She was frightened, but she did never attempt to change the date we had a year before planned for finishing her psychoanalytic treatment.

This new capacity to pause and wait was a new achievement. "Be still and wait", T. S. Eliot's wrote, and I had the idea *that this new stand still somehow lifted the old traumatic halt of 'divalence', which had caused a split in her development.* This former halt had punctuated a period of psychic struggle and had also dissolved some synchronicity of her intellectual and her psycho-sexual progress.

III.

> The end is, where we start from.
> (T. S. Eliot, 1974, 221)

Let us now finally try to distillate some tendencies, which seem to bend the bow from the end of psychoanalytic treatments to their beginnings.

1. The psychoanalytic space – entering and leaving

Entering into an analytic experience means to enter a new space. "The psychoanalytic space becomes the space in which the patient thinks, feels and lives" (Ogden 2011, 183). To enter a new room hardly can be experienced without an emotional response to this change. The reaction might differ in the degree from a light uneasiness, balanced by relief, to a great fear in an emotional storm, as Bion (1987) suggested.

Leaving the couch causes the corresponding feelings, because it is again the change of stepping into an unknown space. Mostly the new freedom is less in the foreground than the mourning of the loss. It is about the loss of the (transference-) object that coloured the psychoanalytic space; both become intimately intertwined. It is an important change, when no longer a certain field is provided for material that presses to return. Th. Ogden wrote: "The termination phase of an analysis is not simply a phase of resolution of conflicted unconscious transference meanings. Equally important, it is a period of *'contraction' of the analytic space* such that the patient comes to experience himself as constituting the space within which he lives and within which the analytic process continues. *If this does not occur*, the prospect of the end of the analysis is experienced as *tantamount to the loss of one's mind or the loss of the space in which one feels alive"* (Ogden 2011, 184). It is the change from analysis terminable to analysis interminable. The termination of psychoanalytic treatment is "a painful wrench for which the word 'mourning' is not too strong" (Green 2002, 45)

The emotional storm of the beginning has its equivalent hurricane of ending.

2. The state of ignorance – decreasing and rising again

Our clinical vignette had shown especially clearly, how at the beginning of analytic treatment the secondary process becomes less effective, while the primary process advances, as soon as there is an outlet for what had been repressed. This phenomenon results in a loss or at least a reduction of control. It will facilitate plenty of parapraxes during the analytic process thus helping to understand what is going on in the realm of the unconscious. It has to do with the de-integrated state "that involves unusual potential for psychological change", as Thomas

Ogden described (Ogden 2011, 187). "The defensive structure that the individual has been relying on is temporarily in a state of flux sufficient to allow him to unconsciously experience himself as having the potential to live differently."

The rather helpless and painful state of ignorance before analysis might change after hard struggles during the analytic process to a state of relative well-being and certainty to have at least some access to unconscious sources of pain and to know some ways of coping with it. However, after the treatment usually there will not be such a large space for devoting oneself to psychic processes in the presence of a well-disposed object. There might even be again a reduction to a lower level of awareness of what is going on. Nevertheless, this does not mean that the analysis was less successful. On the contrary, often those insights are especially effective that were allowed to sink down into the unconscious.

Julian Barnes lent from English poetry a metaphor for the human life that might illustrate also the changes before, during and after psychoanalytic treatment:

> a bird flies out of the darkness
> into an illuminated festival hall
> and leaves the hall again on the other side
> flying into the darkness again

(Barnes 2011, p. 153)

Returning to the original state of darkness/ignorance reminds of an important statement Freud's concerning the transference: the intimacy provided by the patients transference should be lifted at the end of analysis. "The doctor has been a stranger, and must endeavour to become a stranger once more after the cure" (Freud 1907, SE 20, 90). This advice is often neglected causing a lot of problems, especially in psychoanalytic institutes, when relationships between analyst and (former) candidates are loaded with unresolved and uncontrolled transference- and counter-transference feelings. Transference will never totally disappear.

A successful analysis has not to lead to a permanent watching of the psychic processes, but to the capacity which D. Quinodoz described in her paper "Wise enough to dare to be mad at times" (D. Quinodoz 2011, 308 ff.) The emphasis is on "at times", in a similar way as Ogden pointed at the "temporarily" fluent state of the defensive structure. It means that the individual has after the psychoanalytic treatment acquired a possibility to get some access to the unconscious, if it is necessary.[17] Then it is helpful to "know the riddles", as Sophokles put it, in order

---

17 It might be needed, if the primary process seeks discharge not only in dreams, but also for instance in symptoms. However, also creative activities demand access to the unconscious. "In poetry, especially, the proper portion of the two [primary and secondary processes] is crucial" (Akhtar 2009, 221).

to solve the riddle of the Sphinx, or whatever disguise our monstrous fears and wishes will choose (see page 19 in this volume).

It is an advantage, if in the first interview the potential patient's transference does not unfold with the speed of a parachute. Later on, the patient will never have the same chance of a judgement that is closer to a realistic view. Thus, part of the patient's fear regarding *the choice*[18] *of a specific analyst is justified and realistic. (cf. Ogden 2011; Green 2011).*

3. Dialectics constituting psychoanalysis

From the first interview on until to the end of analysis the patient will be confronted with polarities. They might be very confusing at the beginning, and a successful end of the treatment will among many other results show that the analysand has achieved now a greater tolerance for contradictory aspects.

Th. Ogden mentioned already the polarity of "intimacy in the context of formality" (Ogden 2011, p.176) and the "poles of the predictable and the unpredictable" (Ogden 2011, p. 187);

I would like to add some further polarities:

- there is the common "creation of a chimera" (Donnet 2011, 120), of fantasies, which have the function to create a full reality of life (Loewald 1980, 363);
- there is the seemingly unimportant detail, which turns out to be the essential (Bollas 2011) <I remind you once more of our clinical vignette: Susan's minimal delay to the first interview became the nucleus of her problem, that she had not been able to make a choice between a male or a female sexual object. Susan once named me a "soulguard", opposed to a bodyguard. Both professions have in common that they have to pay more attention to hidden and secret processes in the background than to the events that attract the look of the crowd.> About the central meaning of the seemingly unimportant Bollas wrote that deep in his heart Freud estimated the irrelevant much higher than the dark secrets of the analysand (Bollas 2011, p. 12);
- there is the separation created by an interpretation (Donnet 2011, p. 134), that produces intimacy, when the patient allows the analyst to analyse him (Kohon 2005, p. 82),
- and there is the psychoanalytic setting that embodies the inner structure and represents the mind in a dreamlike state (Parsons 1999, p. 64).

---

18 "The choice of an analyst", and the "art of analysis" (Zwettler-Otte 2011b, p. 75 ff.), are in my view *highly underestimated issues.* (Cf. also Zwettler-Otte 2011a, p. 121 ff.)

4. The patient's project at the beginning –
   The patient's project at the end of his analysis

Concluding I would like to have a short look at the initial draft the patient might have made, when he/she started analysis, and compare it with the outlook, the project of the future in the termination phase.

The initial sketches will hardly have the chance of a clear design, since they will be dominated by a compulsion to repeat and to offer the analyst a role that would cause similar situations like those painfully experienced in the past.

There will be another draft designed at the end of analysis regarding the future, a future without being in regular analytic treatment. Many sketches, many movements can be needed to overcome the fear of a transition (Bürgin 2011), and they will probably illustrate the acceptance that there does not exist any certainty how these drafts will develop.

Whatever these final rough drawings will contain, they will probably in some traits approach to the ideal Andrè Green recently dared to sketch:

"a variety, diversity and richness of investments, with a priority for relationships with others;
an absence of rigid fixations and defences;
flexibility and mobility in mental functioning;
the capacity to love and also to hate without allowing oneself to be carried away by a passionate attitude;
the possibility of investing both parental imagos positively as well as close family relations;
a compromise between loving and working that is not too conflictual;
the possibility, when circumstances require it, to go through an experience of mourning without it becoming interminable;
the ability to tolerate disappointments and frustrations, as well as
to recognize the privilege of loving" (Green 2011, p. 98).

References

Amati-Mehler, J. (2011): Realität und Psychose. In Phantasie und Realität – Psychoanalytische Betrachtungen. Ed. Nedelmann C., Stuttgart: Kohlhammer

Akthar, S. (2009): Comprehensiv Dictionary of Psychoanalysis. London: Karnac

Barnes, J. (2011): Nichts, was man fürchten müßte. München: Random-House

Bion, W.R. (1987): Making the best of a bad job. In: Clinical Seminars and four papers. Abingdon: Fleetwood

Bollas, Ch. (2011): Übertragungsdeutung als Widerstand gegen die freie Assoziation. In: Phantasie und Realität – Psychoanalytische Betrachtungen. Ed. Nedelmann C., Stuttgart: Kohlhammer

Bürgin, D. (2011): Zur Theorie und Klinik von Übergangsbewegungen. In: Phantasie und Realität – Psychoanalytische Betrachtungen. Ed. Nedelmann C., Stuttgart: Kohlhammer.
Donnet, L. and M'uzan, M. (2011): The analytic encounter. In: Initiating Psychoanalysis. Perspectives. Ed. Reith B. e. a. New York: Routledge
Eliot, T.S. (1974): East Coker. London: faber and faber
Freud, S. (1907): Delusion and Dream in Jensen's Gradiva, SE 9
Freud, S. (1913): On Beginning the Treatment, SE 12
Freud, S. (1926): The Question of Lay Analysis, SE 20
Green, A. (2002): Time in Psychoanalysis. Some Contradictory Aspects. London: Free Assocoiation Books
Green, A. and Kohon, G. (2005): Love and its Vicissitudes. London: Routledge
Green, A., (Ed.) (2007): Resonance of Suffering. London: The Psychoanalytic Association
Green, A. (2011): Illusions and Disillusions of Psychoanalytic Work. London: Karnac
Hesse, H. (1895-1941): Gesammelte Werke, Band 1
Kohon, G. (1986): The British School of Psychoanalysis. London: Free Association Books.
Kohon, G. (Ed.) (1999): The Dead Mother. London: Routledge
Kohon, G. (1999): No Lost Certainties to be Recovered. London: Karnac
Kohon, G. (2007): Borderline Traces and the Question of Diagnosis. In: Green, A., Ed.: Resonance of Suffering. London: The Psychoanalytic Association
Kohon, G. (2010): Amore nel transfert. Identificazione primaria e imago materna. In: Psicoanalisi. Revista della Associazione Italiana di Psicoanalisi. Ed. Amati-Mehler J. Milano: Franco Angeli
Ogden, Th. (2011): Comments on transference and countertransference in the initial analytic meeting. In: Initiating Psychoanalysis. – Perspectives. Ed. Reith, B. e. a. New York: Routledge
Parsons, M. (1999): Psychic reality, negation, and the analytic setting. In: The Dead Mother. Ed. Kohon, G. London: Routledge
Quinodoz, D. (2011): The psychoanalyst of the future: Wise enough to dare to be mad at times. In: Initiating Psychoanalysis. – Perspectives. Ed. Reith B. e. a., New York: Routledge
Sandler, J., Sandler, A.-M. (1998): Internal Objects revisited. London: Karnac
Schwab, G. (1978): Der Reiter und der Bodensee. In: Deutscher Balladenschatz. Bayreuth: Gondron Verlag

Wegner, P. (2011): The opening scene and the importance of the countertransference in the initial psychoanalytic interview. In: Initiating Psychoanalysis. – Perspectives. Ed. Reith, B. e. a., New York: Routledge

Zwettler-Otte, S. (2011 a): The Melody of Separation: A Psychoanalytic Study on Separation-Anxiety. Frankfurt-Berlin-Oxford-Wien: Peter Lang

Zwettler-Otte, S. (2011 b): Ebbe und Flut – Gezeiten des Eros. Psychoanalytische Gedanken und Fallstudien über die Liebe. Stuttgart: Kohlhammer

About the authors

Stefano Bolognini
Stefano Bolognini is Training Analyst in Bologna and is president of the Italian Psychoanalytic Society and president-elect of the International Psychoanalytical Association.
Among his books, some published in English are:
"*Psychoanalytic Empathy*". Free Association (2004)
"*Like Wind, Like Wave*", Other Press, New York, 2006.
"*Secret Passages*". IPA New Library, Routledge, London, 2010.

Alain Gibeault, PH.D.
Philosopher, psychologist and psychoanalyst, Alain Gibeault is a Training Analyst of the Paris Psychoanalytical Society and Director of the E.&J. Kestemberg Centre for Psychoanalysis and Psychotherapy (Mental Health Association of Paris 13th). He has played an important role on the international scene as Past President of the European Psycho-Analytical Federation and as Past Secretary General of the International Psychoanalytical Association. In this function he has contributed to the development of psychoanalysis in Eastern Europe after the fall of the Berlin wall and especially in Russia, where he has been nominated in November 2006 Honorary Professor of the Lomonossov Moscow State University. He is now the chair of the IPA Allied Centres Committee, which are helping health professionals to develop psychoanalysis in countries where there are no or only few psychoanalysts; he is presently working with colleagues of the Mediterranean countries (Maghreb) and of the Middle East (Iran).

He is the co-editor of an Anthology of French psychoanalysis in Russian published in 2004; an Anthology of British psychoanalysis is now under preparation. Well known for his publications on symbolization, he has published many writings on psychosis, on the theory and technique of individual psychoanalytic psychodrama and on prehistoric art. He has published in January 2010 with Dana Birksted-Breen and Sara Flanders an anthology of French psychoanalytic papers entitled *Reading French Psychoanalysis* (Routledge) and in July 2010 a book entitled *Chemins de la symbolisation* (Presses Universitaires de France).

Rainer Gross, Dr. med.
Psychiatrist (Head of the psychiatric department at Landeskrankenhaus Hollabrunn near Vienna) and psychoanalyst in private practice in Vienna. Member of the Viennese Psychoanalytic Society (WPV-IPA).

Publications (in German) on the topic of application of psychodynamic concepts in psychiatric practice and on psychoanalysis and reception of art (literature, film).

Recent publications:
„Geschichten: Immer traurig, teilweise sehr hübsch" – Die Figur der Hysterikerin in der (Populär-)Kultur des Fin de siècle
„Angewandte" Psychoanalyse: Sigmund Freud, seine "Libido-Spürhunde" und "wild gewordene Neurosensuche"
Das Bild des Psychoanalytikers, das Bild der Psychoanalyse
All three papers in: Zwettler-Otte, S. (Hrsg.): „Durch 1000 Kanäle und Poren ..." Die Verbreitung der Psychoanalyse von ihren Anfängen bis zur Gegenwart. Frankfurt/Main 2009: Peter Lang Verlag
Der Psychotherapeut im Film. Stuttgart 2012: Kohlhammer-Verlag
Angst, Depression und die Verleugnung von Abhängigkeit: Ein Essay In: Österreichische Zeitschrift für Soziologie, Jg. 37/Heft 4/2012, S. 439-453.

Sylvia Zwettler-Otte, Mag. Dr.
Born and living in Vienna, Austria, she took her degrees in Latin, German and Psychology at the University of Vienna in 1968 and 1975. She participated in several projects of the Viennese Sigmund Freud- Society, among these a nearly ten years lasting project together with a historian about the early reception of psychoanalysis and Sigmund Freud in the printings 1895-1938. The results of this research were published in German 1999: Freud in der Presse. Die Rezeption der Psychoanalyse 1895-1938, (edited with Marina Tichy, Vienna, Sonderzahl.) 2006 a short English version was published: Freud and the Media – The Reception of Psychoanalysis in Viennese Medical Journals 1895-1938, (Peter Lang-Europäischer Verlag der Wissenschaften, Frankfurt).

She works in full-time private practice and is a training analyst of the Viennese Psychoanalytic Society (WPV/IPA). Since 1992 she is a member of the Viennese Psychoanalytic Society; 1996 – 2004 she was a member of the Board and 2000- 2004 president of the Viennese Psychoanalytic Society. She teaches at the Viennese Psychoanalytic Academy.

She published several psychoanalytic books in German; another one translated into English is

The Melody of separation. A psychoanalytic study on separation-anxiety: (Peter Lang-Internationaler Verlag der Wissenschaften).

Figures

Figure 1:   Man-buffalo, Chauvet Cave, 32000 BP © Yanik Le Guillou
Figure 2:   Scene of the well, Lascaux cave, 17000 BP © A. Glory
Figure 3:   Martha Bernays and Sigmund Freud 1885, in G. Henning: Sigmund Freud – Eine Bildbiographie, Köln: Taschen Verlag
Figure 4:   Freud-medal, photo by S.Zwettler-Otte
Figure 5:   Vienna, University, Arcades, photo by H. Wolfgruber
Figure 6:   University-Arcades, corner with Freud's bust, photo by H. Wolfgruber
Figure 7:   Arcades, Freud's bust, photo by S. Zwettler-Otte
Figure 8:   Greek inscription on Freud's bust, photo by S. Zwettler-Otte
Figure 9:   Sphinx from Freud's collection, photo in: Gamwell + Wells 1989
Figure 10: Greek winged Sphinx, photo from: Demisch 1977
Figure 11: Oedipus killing the sphinx by club, photo from: Demisch 1977
Figure 12: Oedipus before the Sphinx (Greek vase), photo from: Demisch 1977
Figure 13: Khnopff, Fernand: Oedipus and the Sphinx, photo from: Symbolismus, Köln: Taschen-Verlag 2011
Figure 14: Sphinx-Collage by Clarence Sinclair Bull, 1931, in: Greta Garbo – Das private Album, hrsg. Scott Reisfield, Robert Dance, Berlin: Henschel Verlag 2005

www.ingramcontent.com/pod-product-compliance
Ingram Content Group UK Ltd.
Pitfield, Milton Keynes, MK11 3LW, UK
UKHW021259180426
11947UKWH00015B/930